BIBLICAL
SEPARATION
DEFENDED

A Biblical Critique
Of Ten New Evangelical Arguments

By

GARY G. COHEN

The Presbyterian and Reformed Publishing Co.

Philadelphia, Pa.

1966

PHOTOLITHOPRINTED BY CUSHING - MALLOY, INC.
ANN ARBOR, MICHIGAN, UNITED STATES OF AMERICA
1966

PUBLISHER'S NOTE

This monograph by Gary G. Cohen, a member of the faculty of Faith Theological Seminary at Philadelphia, deals with but one aspect of Dr. Billy Graham's ministry — that of "cooperative evangelism." It is specifically concerned to refute the basic thesis of Dr. Robert O. Ferm in his *Cooperative Evangelism: Is Billy Graham Right or Wrong?* that "cooperative evangelism" as practiced by Dr. Graham is the method taught in Scripture. We are well aware that Dr. Graham is the leading Christian evangelist of our day. We, as well as Mr. Cohen, praise the Lord for the souls that have been saved in the Graham crusades. However, in this particular area of methodology we feel that the "cooperative evangelists" are in error. God's work is to be done in God's way. When God's work is not done in His way, then both good and evil are produced. Those who run in His race must run according to His rules if they expect to receive the prize, because a "man is not crowned except he have contended lawfully" (II Tim. 2:5).

It should be kept in mind that Mr. Cohen uses the term "fundamentalist" in a sense that would include those generally spoken of as "conservative." In other words he equates "fundamentalism" with historical and/or Biblical Christianity and uses the terms "liberals" and "modernists" to denote those whose theological views cannot be reconciled with Christianity rightly so called. This is not to deny that there are liberals who could be characterized as more or less badly deformed types of Christians. This observation in no way lessens the thrust of Mr. Cohen's argument. In fact, the influence on new converts of prominent liberals who hold views of the Bible, the atonement, the miraculous, etc., which are not consistent with Christianity — even though they themselves may actually have a saving faith in Christ — may well be more harmful than that of those who obviously are not among the saints.

Mr. Cohen has quoted from Dr. Ferm's *Cooperative Evangelism: Is Billy Graham Right or Wrong?* only so far as is necessary to analyze his position. We suggest that the interested reader secure a copy of this book, published by the Zondervan Publishing Company of Grand Rapids, Michigan, for a more comprehensive study of this point of view.

CONTENTS

INTRODUCTION

Statement of Purpose

This book is offered to the Christian public with the hope that it will answer ten arguments which have been spread across our nation even unto the lands beyond the seas. These ten arguments claim that it is both Biblical and right for true Christians who believe their Bible to cooperate in doing the work of the Lord with those who, while traveling under the title of "Christian," deny the inspiration of the Scriptures, the virgin birth of Christ, His bodily resurrection, and the like.

The ten arguments here analyzed are to be heard today in seminary halls, churches, and across a myriad of Christian living rooms. They are championed by those who are called, "New Evangelicals"—for these cry constantly that the right way to evangelize the lost is a "new" way, i.e., one in which the cooperation of those who disbelieve the fundamentals of the Historic Christian Faith is welcomed and even sought out. Thus "Cooperative [with liberal and neo-orthodox theologians] Evangelism" is the mode of winning the lost which they advocate.

While the ten arguments which form the subject of this work are found on the lips of men and women in every Christian walk of life—puzzling some, attracting others—I have thought it best to study them as they are actually advocated in written form by one New Evangelical author. This seemed better than to constantly claim, "They say . . .," without being able to point to one unified source for my claims. Therefore, I have selected as a representative spokesman of this group, Dr. Robert O. Ferm, and I have considered ten of the claims which he makes in his widely circulated book, *Cooperative Evangelism: Is Billy Graham Right or Wrong?*[1]

Since the field was so vast, I have further limited this critique to an examination of the New Evangelical arguments based upon

---

1. Robert O. Ferm, *Cooperative Evangelism: Is Billy Graham Right or Wrong?* (Grand Rapids: Zondervan Publishing House, 1958), pp. 11-23, 33-47.

the ministry of the Lord Jesus Christ. The reader, however, will, by the time he finishes this study, see that the same principles apply equally well to the ministries and epistles of Paul and the other apostles. The case for New Evangelicals versus Ecclesiastical Separation can well be fought to a complete finish here on the battlefield of the Gospels. It need go no further. The result is decisive! Let the reader judge for himself.

Importance of the Basic Problem

The ranks of the orthodox have been divided! This division which separates evangelicals into two camps has been created by two distinct and opposite views on the relationship of true orthodox Christians to modernists and liberals. The separatists see in the Bible the clear teaching that God's work is to be done exclusively by born again doctrinally sound people, and that modernist clergymen are heretics, enemies of the Gospel, and ought to have no part in the Lord's work, but must be separated from, rebuked, and warned against openly. In contrast to this view neo-evangelicals hold that liberals may have a part in the preaching of the conservative Gospel, may be approached with a friendly attitude by believers, and are not to be viewed so much as heretics. Instead they are to be looked at merely as those who intellectually hold views somewhat divergent from their more conservative brethren. This difference is so extreme and fundamental that the biblically commanded conduct and posture of believers toward unbelievers is seen by each of the two parties to be the opposite advocated by the other. The question is, "Shall modernistic false teachers be treated as friends or enemies of the Church of Jesus Christ?"

With the ever rising tide of liberalism, evolution, Communism, Socialism, the Social Gospel, and unbelief in the United States and in the world at large, it is more essential now than ever before that the correct behavior by fundamentalists towards modernism be ascertained. The fundamentalists claim that separation is the only answer to modernism, while the neo-evangelicals see a policy of cooperation with liberals and its alleged resultant increased spread of the Gospel as the answer. The future of

Christianity humanly speaking depends upon the Church's making the correct decision on this matter and, since the alternatives are in opposite directions, the wrong choice, if adopted by the majority of the orthodox Church, could bring ruin upon it with frightening rapidity.

The correct view in the opinion of the writer, which is set forth at the end of this study, is seen in the words of an Old Testament passage which is centered about the verse, 2 Chronicles 19:2. The situation sees Jehu, God's righteous prophet, rebuking Jehoshaphat, a man of God who erred by forming an alliance with wicked Ahab, God's enemy. Jehoshaphat aided the enemy of God and, despite his other righteous acts, this was a grave sin which harmed the Lord's cause. This so well fits the New Evangelicals of today who are wrongly cooperating with the modernists while thinking to themselves that they are advancing the cause of Judah. May the words of God, spoken through the mouth of Jehu the separatist prophet, thunder in their ears and reach their hearts.

> And Jehu the son of Hanani the seer went out to meet him, and said to king Jehoshaphat, Shouldest thou help the ungodly, and love them that hate the LORD? therefore is wrath upon thee from before the LORD.
> Nevertheless there are good things found in thee, in that thou hast taken away the groves out of the land, and hast prepared thine heart to seek God. (2 Chron. 19:2,3)[2]

The aim of this work is to advance the truth of the message of Jehu to all of those in God's family.

Dr. Ferm's Book

Dr. Ferm, in his book *Cooperative Evangelism: Is Billy Graham Right or Wrong?*, defends the inclusivist methods of cooperative evangelism by observations and conclusions from five primary areas. These are: (1) the ministry of the Lord,

---

2. This scripture and all succeeding ones have been taken from the Authorized Version (1611) unless otherwise noted.

(2) the ministries of the non-Pauline apostles as noted in the book of Acts, (3) the ministry of the Apostle Paul, (4) the proof texts, chiefly Pauline, most often cited by separatists, and (5) the practice of the most famous modern day evangelists, Whitefield, Wesley, Finney, Moody, and Sunday.[3] The first four of these areas are biblically orientated, while the fifth, to which the most pages are devoted, is historically orientated.

Although the Bible is referred to throughout Dr. Ferm's short book of five chapters, the third chapter, "Cooperative Evangelism and the New Testament," is the chapter in which Dr. Ferm analyzes the ministries of the Lord, Paul, and the other apostles, as well as the proof texts. Omitting the one page treatment of the other apostles which is negligible, the examination of the New Testament covers the three primary areas of the ministries of Paul, the Lord, plus the section on proof texts.[4] In each of these sections Dr. Ferm enumerates divers incidents and texts, and alleges that they show the Lord or Paul to have favored the policy of Cooperative Evangelism rather than the policy of separatism. As mentioned above, and for the reasons indicated, we will content ourselves with an analysis of the section dealing with the ministry of our Lord.

Although *Cooperative Evangelism* received its first printing in April, 1958, of 15,000 copies, it was received with such enthusiasm in evangelical circles as a defense of the neo-evangelical type of inclusivist evangelism, such as practiced by Billy Graham, that more printings were shortly demanded.[5] This concise study based on the New Testament and the practices of the great evangelists of the past two centuries, made available for the low price of seventy-five cents per copy, and a dozen copies for only seven dollars and twenty cents, by the end of June, 1958, had seen its fourth printing which brought the total number of volumes in print to the huge number of 75,000.[6] It was sent to religious colleges and seminaries and to many clergymen free of charge by

---

3. Ferm, p. 48.

4. *Ibid.*, pp. 33-47.

5. *Ibid.*, p. 6.

6. *Ibid.*

parties interested in spreading its message—that Cooperative Evangelism is justified biblically and historically, as well as pragmatically. Dr. Donald A. Waite, Professor of Speech at Shelton College, then in Ringwood, New Jersey, told the writer of this thesis that while he was a Navy Chaplain on far away Okinawa in the Pacific, he received by mail a complimentary copy of *Cooperative Evangelism*.[7] This is one example of the widespread circulation of Dr. Ferm's work throughout the Protestant clerical community.

It is unfortunate that conservative laymen and pastors are told in this work that cooperative evangelism, not separated evangelism, is the method taught in the Scriptures. In view of this book's wide circulation and in view of the current theological climate, which sees neo-evangelicalism and separatism each striving to justify their antagonistic positions on the basis of the Bible, this book needs to be answered.

Clarifications

At no time should this book ever be thought to attack Dr. Ferm's personality, integrity, or his desire to serve Jesus Christ; nor should it ever be construed to question his motive for thinking as he does. The only thing that is here in question is his examination and findings concerning the ministry of the Lord. This, however, is no light subject, and if Dr. Ferm is in error concerning cooperative evangelism, then considering that 75,000 copies of his book are in circulation, this is a grievous error despite the fact of Dr. Ferm's sincerity.

As the volume at issue has as its full title the words, *Cooperative Evangelism: Is Billy Graham Right or Wrong?*, it is clearly a defense of Dr. Graham's basic evangelistic policy. Therefore, a critique of Dr. Ferm's words and his policies on evangelism happens in most cases to be a critique of Dr. Graham's policies and methods. However, the aim of this work is not to examine

---

7. Interview with Dr. Donald A. Waite, April 17, 1963.

per se Dr. Graham, and all references to him are to be understood as subservient to the main task at hand.[8]

It is also plainly to be understood that where Dr. Ferm is criticized for his arguments in favor of liberal sponsorship of meetings where a conservative gospel is to be preached, that the writer never intends to imply that no conservative also participates in the sponsorship. It is fully realized that evangelicals do participate in the sponsorship of the meetings. The question at issue, however, is whether liberals ought to be among the sponsors at all, and the dominating element at that.

It is also to be realized that the writer as well as separatists everywhere praise the Lord for the many souls that have been saved in the Graham crusades, despite the fact that the writer sees clearly taught in the Scriptures the doctrine of Ecclesiastical Separation. The writer, however, laments the fact that so many of today's evangelicals with all their scholarship have not yet learned the simple truth, that God's work is to be done in God's way. When God's work is not done in God's way, then both good and evil are produced, and only He who sees all things from His seat in heaven can see on which side the balance leans.

Although this study takes to task a defense of what it believes to be an unbiblical type of evangelism, and may often point out the need for defending the faith, an antithesis between the two is not to be conceived. The writer believes in biblical evangelism's absolute importance and in the necessity for fulfilling the Great Commission of Matthew 28:19,20, but the exposition of this theme is not the subject of this inquiry. However, because the necessity of evangelism is not here stressed, the writer wishes all readers to realize that they are not forced to choose between defending the faith or winning the lost, for both are Scriptural imperatives, and both are to be performed in God's way.

---

8. It is also worth noting at this point that Dr. Ferm is presently the Team Coordinator for the Billy Graham Evangelistic Association. This further clarifies the close relationship between Dr. Ferm's book and Dr. Graham's policies.

GROUP ONE

ARGUMENTS ADVOCATING COOPERATION
WITH SO-CALLED NON-OPPONENTS

ARGUMENT I

"Christ Instructed the Twelve and the Seventy
to Lodge with Anyone Who Was Willing
to Have Them."

The Argument Advanced by Dr. Ferm

The first argument to be challenged is one concerning the sending forth of the twelve disciples, and later, the seventy disciples, to proclaim the Kingdom of God (Matt. 10:1-42; Luke 9:1-6; 10:1-16). Here Dr. Ferm declares that the Lord instructed the twelve and the seventy to cooperate with any who, after being aware of their message, would have them; and they were only to leave a house when positively rejected.[1] Therefore, it is held, modern evangelists ought to cooperate with any person or group who, after being made aware of their message, will have them; and they ought to refuse to cooperate only when either (1) their message is limited, or (2) they are positively rejected.[2]

Dr. Ferm defends his view by claiming that when Christ sent out the Twelve on an evangelistic mission "they were supposed to accept hospitality when it was offered. They were to leave only when they were positively rejected" (Matthew 10:14).[3] He likewise claims that when our Lord sent out the Seventy in Luke 10:5-10 to proclaim that the kingdom of God is come that they were given "instructions to enter into any community or home that would receive them, but on their own terms."[4]

---

1. *Ibid.*, pp. 34-35.
2. *Ibid.*
3. *Ibid.*, p. 34.
4. *Ibid.*, pp. 34-35.

1

An Examination of Dr. Ferm's Conclusions

Dr. Ferm has gathered from the passages in question that it is permissible for a conservative to cooperate in the proclamation of the Gospel with anyone who while being aware of the conservative message to be proclaimed will cooperate, be he a modernist or not. Dr. Ferm contends also that this is the method advocated by the Lord. In fact, he declares, it is not even the responsibility of the evangelist to determine the motives which may have prompted a believer in evolution or a denier of the atonement to invite a conservative preacher to come.[5] Thus the criterion for cooperation deduced by Dr. Ferm is solely the *willingness* of a host who is aware of the orthodox message to be proclaimed. "On the contrary," says Dr. Ferm, the evangelist "is more closely conforming to the scriptural pattern by going to those who have the greater spiritual need, as long as he declares to them the whole counsel of God."[6]

The Writer's Critique

Amid the Lord's instructions to the twelve in Matthew 10:11 the expression, "Search out who in it is worthy," is found. Since these words are in the best manuscripts, there are no textual problems involved in them.[7] The Greek verb, *exetazo*, translated "search out," according to Arndt and Gingrich's Lexicon means, "1. *Scrutinize, examine, inquire, make a careful search for someone; 2. Question, examine, someone . . . Question* judicially, esp. in connection with torture."[8] The word *axios*, "worthy," appears seven times in Matthew 10 alone, and when it refers to persons, as in the case at hand, it means "worthy," and "fit."[9] It is difficult perhaps to determine the exact and full implications of these words, but certain extremes can be eliminated and a degree of certainty

---

5. *Ibid.*, p. 39.

6. *Ibid.*, p. 35.

7. Eberhard Nestle, *et al.* (editors). *Novum Testamentum* Graece (23rd ed.; Stuttgart: Privileg. Wurt., 1957), *in loc.*, Matt. 10:11.

8. William F. Arndt and F. Wilbur Gingrich, *A Greek-English Lexicon of the New Testament and Other Early Christian Literature* (Chicago: University of Chicago Press, 1957), p. 275.

9. *Ibid.*, p. 77.

can be apprehended. The *searching out* of the *worthy* host could not be referring to a prolonged extensive investigation involving repeated interviews and committee consultations. The contextual circumstances and the time factor would prohibit this. However, a *searching out* of a *worthy* party clearly is commanded and this carries with it the unmistakable implication that certain homes were unworthy.

What are the criteria for worthiness that the context would seem to call for? One criterion would no doubt be a house that would not give offense to the townspeople, and so retard the new religious thrust. Would the home of a friendly gentile sorcerer or idol worshiper hinder the proclamation by the twelve that "The Kingdom of Heaven is at hand?" It would not only hinder it, it would annihilate it! Or suppose that there was a profiteer in the town, whose greed the townspeople despised, who for the sake of additional hotel revenue decided that he would like to play host to the new movement. Would a willingness on this man's part be sufficient criterion for the disciples to conduct their crusade *under his auspices* as Dr. Ferm's sole criterion of *willingness* would allow? It can be seen that *willingness* alone is not a sufficient standard, for the entire thrust of the disciple's proclamation could be given a ruinous bad name by the wrong associations. If Paul thought it important enough to have Titus circumcised in order to remove an unnecessary stumbling block from the minds of the Jews among whom he was about to minister, surely the Lord would not consent to a sorcerer's willingness as a sufficient reason for basing His proclamation headquarters at a local temple of idols. Who can deny that if the twelve lodged with any such person or group, it would so mar the reputation of the twelve, their message, and their master that it would be virtually impossible for them to obtain a hearing in Jewry, let alone achieve success! The Lord's concern for the reputation and testimony of His disciples, His message, and His own name is probably one of the prime reasons for His forbidding His disciples from going from house to house (Matt. 10:11; Luke 10:8); for not only would this procedure be unsettling to the disciples in their work, but also it might appear to the people that the disciples were travelling from home to home to get whatever they could from each house. The same idea is expressed in 1

3

Timothy 3:7, "Moreover he [one who desires the office of a Bishop] must have a good report of them which are without; lest he fall into reproach and the snare of the devil." Thus it is inescapably seen that Dr. Ferm's interpretation of this passage, in which he sees *willingness* to be the sole standard, is inadequate and it does not take into consideration Matthew 10:11 which requires the disciples to "Search out who in it [the city] is worthy."

Not only would idol worshipers, sorcerers, and profiteers be considered as not "worthy" but in Luke 10:10-16 in the discourse to the Seventy, unbelievers are so castigated by the Lord that they surely must be outside of the "worthy" class. "Woe unto thee, Chorazin! Woe unto thee, Bethsaida! for if the mighty works had been done in Tyre and Sidon, which were done in you, they would have repented long ago, . . ." (Luke 10:13). This has a different ring to it than Ferm's words,

> The problem becomes exceedingly complex when one's associations are with nominal Christians, especially when they manifest the Christian graces, yet cannot intellectually accept every tenet of Fundamentalism. By what standard must one decide to separate from such persons?[10]

Unbelief according to a reasonable exegesis of Luke 10:1-16 removed a person from the worthy class. When one realizes that the tenets of fundamentalism, of which Dr. Ferm speaks, are the foundations of the faith, and not the denominational distinctive frills, one understands that those who "cannot intellectually accept every tenet of fundamentalism" such as the Substitutionary Atonement, the Virgin Birth, and the Bodily Resurrection, are the very unbelievers that the Lord addressed in Chorazin, with only the time and setting changed.

Who then is "worthy"? The righteous and pious believers can be the only answer! This best accords with the usage of the word "worthy" (*axios*) in passages such as Revelation 3:4, "And they shall walk with me in white for they are worthy." Did the disciples

---

10. Ferm, p. 34.

4

understand and the Lord imply that this was to be one who already loved Christ or merely a pious Jew who while looking for the Messiah had not yet heard of the Nazarene called, "Jesus"? Perhaps this cannot be known, but in Matthew 10:11 a pious or righteous man, who had a godly reputation, is the least that can be undstood to be implied in the word "worthy."

In Matthew 7:15 Christ said, "Beware of false prophets, which come to you in sheep's clothing, but inwardly they are ravening wolves." These words would certainly eliminate "false prophets" from the list of worthy men; and the twelve could not consent to be "sponsored" by one who had the reputation of being a false prophet merely on the grounds that the false prophet was *willing* to have them even after being aware of the message which they were going to proclaim. If they did so, they would be directly violating Matthew 7:15, "Beware of false prophets"; Matthew 10:16, "Behold, I send you forth as sheep in the midst of wolves: be ye therefore as wise as serpents, and harmless as doves"; and Matthew 10:11, "And into whatsoever city or town ye shall enter, enquire who in it is worthy; and there abide until ye go thence."

Matthew 10:11, the verse just quoted, with the command, "Inquire," being in the Aorist Imperative, placed upon the disciples the responsibility of determining as much as possible the reasons which prompted their host to invite them. If this be applied to today's situation, as Dr. Ferm applies the passage, then if language has any meaning at all, Dr. Ferm's statement, "It cannot be his [any evangelist's] responsibility to determine the motives that prompted their [the liberal sponsors'] invitation,"[11] is the exact opposite of what Matthew 10:11 teaches. In any event, since motives of the liberals are often known, it is at least the evangelist's responsibility not to disregard them.

Dr. Ferm's quotation of Dean Alford in the context of the Lord's words to the Seventy, "Into whatsoever city ye enter, and they receive you, eat such things as are set before you" (Luke 10:8), is remarkable. He quotes and comments:

---

11. *Ibid.,* p. 39.

Dean Alford commented on the word "receiveth" and insisted that it had a broader meaning than merely offering room and board. He said, "It implies a receiving into the heart and life the messenger and his message. The implication of the words of Jesus is that any one who is aware of the beliefs and convictions of the messenger of the Lord, and receives him as such a messenger, is actually receiving the Lord though not in the sense of personal salvation.[12]

Certainly liberals who question the historicity of the bodily resurrection of Christ and who question the substitutionary atonement are the very last people who could be referred to as, "Receiving into the heart and life the messenger and his message," and these who have rejected the foundations of the faith come closer to the category of merely giving the conservative evangelist "room and board" in exchange for a religious emphasis and some new members to their unsound churches.

Concerning Dr. Ferm's words,

. . . On the contrary, he [the evangelist] is more closely conforming to the scriptural pattern by going to those who have the greater spiritual need, as long as he declares to them the whole counsel of God.[13]

it must be noted that the "scriptural pattern" of "going to those who have the greater spiritual need," is a pattern of taking the message of God which can meet the need to those sinners who so desperately require it. It is not one of going to "those who have the greater spiritual need" in order to cooperate with *them* in helping *other* needy ones. Although Matthew 7:5 is set in a context which deals with those who are censorious, the words, "First cast out the beam out of thine own eye; and then shalt thou see clearly to cast out the mote out of thy brother's eye," sets forth a truism which is applicable here. That truism is that the blind are in no position to lead other blind people (cf. Matt. 15:14). Thus the scriptural pattern is for the seeing physician to enlist the aid of

12. *Ibid.*, p. 38.
13. *Ibid.*, p. 35.

6

others with sight to help him give sight to the blind; and it is not one in which the seeing physician looks in the direction of the blind leaders in order to obtain workers to aid in giving others sight. Since Dr. Ferm declares that, "The theological liberal of today is one who has never known the biblical view of the Christian faith," he acknowledges that todays liberals are at best "blind leaders."[14] Therefore, how can they be utilized in helping the blind, for Christ has said, "And if the blind lead the blind, both shall fall into the ditch" (Matt. 15:14). Thus it is seen that Dr. Ferm's conception of the scriptural pattern is erroneous, and that the evangelist is to go "to those who have the greater spiritual need" in order to give aid, not to obtain aid!

Further on the statement above by Dr. Ferm, his words, "as long as he [the evangelist] declares to them the whole counsel of God," contain an extremely weighty misapprehension. This misapprehension is that a conservative evangelist can come to a crusade under liberal sponsorship and yet declare the whole counsel of God to the people. A sponsoree comes under a tacit and understood agreement not to do or say anything that is detrimental to the sponsor. Thus when Dr. Ferm declares, "Whatever their [the sponsor's] own views may be [liberal, etc.], they are extending an invitation to him [Dr. Graham] to proclaim a message that is characteristic of previous crusades," he is uttering the fact that when a liberal group sponsors Dr. Graham, they are extending an invitation to him to preach the same crusade message, which means that there will be no warning given to the people concerning the dangers of falling prey to the modernists, liberals, false prophets, and ravening wolves.[15] Therefore, a conservative is not able to declare the whole counsel of God when under the sponsorship of liberals, and therefore, Dr. Ferm has erred by declaring something to be habitual which in reality is non-existent and impossible.

---

14. *Ibid.*, p. 21.
15. *Ibid.*, p. 39.

Conclusions

It may be questioned as to what principles have application to today's contemporary evangelistic scene from the Lord's in-instructions to the twelve in Matthew 10:11 - 11:1 and its parallel passages, and to the seventy, in Luke 10:1-16. Certainly Matthew 10:21, "And the brother shall deliver up the brother to death, . . ." and the verses around it describe persecutions which extended far beyond the immediate mission of the twelve, and which extend into the post-resurrection proclamation of the Gospel. Nevertheless, it has been seen that Dr. Ferm's interpretation of these passages and his application to modern events, in which he sees in them (1) the Lord instructing the twelve and the seventy to abide with any who satisfy a single criterion of being *willing* to have them while being aware of their message, and (2) warrant for modern-day evangelists to cooperate with any who being aware of their message are *willing* to have them, is not able to be sustained. Dr. Ferm's interpretation and application has omitted the taking into consideration the inquiry for the *worthy* man in Matthew 10:11. His interpretation has neglected the fact that it is an imperative for the proclaiming disciple to undertake this inquiry, and that in light of the Lord's words concerning false prophets and concerning the unbelief in Chorazin and Beth-saida, an unbelieving liberal could not qualify as the worthy man with whom the preaching disciple is to abide.

Dr. Ferm's remarks to the effect that the scriptural pattern ·is for a conservative evangelist to go to liberals in spiritual need for aid in proclaiming the message of hope has been shown to be false. His assertion which implied the ability of a conservative to declare the whole counsel of God when under liberal sponsorship has likewise been shown to be contrary to reality.

Thus Dr. Ferm's first proposition cannot be sustained upon investigation and its usage as an argument for cooperative evangelism, as opposed to a biblically separated evangelism which houses itself in the worthy man's abode, is completely nullified.

ARGUMENT II

"The Lord Accepted the Cooperation of Any Who Did Not Oppose Him"

The Argument Advanced by Dr. Ferm

The second argument of the New Evangelicals affirms that the Lord accepted the cooperation of any who did not oppose him, and therefore, today's evangelists dare not make greater demands.[1] Hence, *Liberals do not oppose the Lord Jesus Christ.*[2]

Dr. Ferm defends the above ideas which he advances by an illusion to the encounter in Luke 9:49-50 wherein Christ chided the apostles for rebuking one who, while being outside the apostolic circle, was nevertheless casting out demons in the name of Christ. From this Dr. Ferm concludes the following:

> If Jesus accepted the cooperation of any who did not oppose him, even though they did not conduct their mission in precisely the same manner he conducted his, an evangelist can scarcely make more exacting demands.[3]

An Examination of Dr. Ferm's Conclusions

Dr. Ferm's own conclusions are mirrored in the issues which his words have raised. He apparently in this case defines the word "oppose" as meaning something akin to "to actively and vocally denounce publicly." His statements indicate that he has concluded from the Luke 9:49-50 passage concerning the "forbidding" and from the rest of the New Testament that the Lord accepted cooperation from any who did not openly oppose him. Dr. Ferm's words, "Even though they did not conduct their mission *in precisely the same manner* he conducted his,"[4] (italics mine) implies that he has concluded that the dispute between

---

1. *Ibid.*, p. 38.
2. Cf. Ferm, pp. 22,38.
3. Ferm, p. 38.
4. *Ibid.*

Cooperative Evangelism and Separatism is one over method, and not one involving a fundamental orientation to the concept of the purity of the Church and the Church's treatment of heretics commanded by a Holy God who *hates unbelief*. However, the fundamental conclusion of Dr. Ferm, upon which the others rest, seems inescapably to be that liberals do not actually *oppose* Christ! His argument that today's conservative evangelists may work with anyone who does not oppose Jesus can favor his cause only if liberals do not oppose Jesus.

The Writer's Critique

His basis for the conclusion that liberals do not *oppose* the Lord Jesus may lie in the fact that he claims, "The theological liberal of today is one who has never known the biblical view of the Christian faith. He is unlike those who opened their attack on the Bible more than half a century ago."[5] He seems to see the liberals as impartial intellectual neutralists who not knowing "the biblical view of the Christian faith" do not believe, and who "unlike those who opened their attack on the Bible more than half a century ago" do not *oppose*, i.e., openly denounce the Christ of the Bible. Of course it is hard to believe that theological liberals who have spent countless hours in and around the Scriptures have never known the biblical view of the Christian faith, except experientially, for they surely know the creed of biblical Christianity which they refuse. On Dr. Ferm's other point, the reason why many liberals are not daily attacking the truth and historicity of the fundamentals of the Christian faith is because they believe that the war is already over and past, and that they by carrying the majority have won in the "old" fundamentalist-modernist controversy of the nineteen-thirties! Tyrants who would bomb cities, were they not already thought by them to have been destroyed, are not to be considered as lovers of peace.

Perhaps the first major item that should be examined in detail in the light of Scripture is Dr. Ferm's words, "If Jesus accepted the cooperation of any who did not oppose him, . . ."[6] Dr.

---

5. Ferm, p. 21.
6. *Ibid.*, p. 38.

Ferm's primary evidence for the truth of this statement is found in the Lord's commanding the twelve not to forbid the man who had been casting out demons in the name of Christ. Certain characteristics about this man should be noticed, however, before the generalization that this man is "any man" dare be made.

Luke relates the happening thus in Luke 9:49-50,

> And John answered and said, Master, we saw one casting out devils [i.e., demons] in thy name; and we forbade him, because he followed not with us. And Jesus said unto him, Forbid him not: for he that is not against us is for us.[7]

About this man Calvin notes:

> Hence it is evident that the *name* of Christ was at that time so celebrated, that persons who were not of the number of his intimate disciples used that *name*, or perhaps even abused it, for I wil not venture to avouch any thing on this point as certain. It is possible that he who is here mentioned had embraced the doctrine of Christ, and betaken himself to the performance of miracles with no bad intention; but as Christ bestowed this power on none but those whom he had chosen to be heralds of his Gospel, I think he had rashly taken, or rather seized upon, this office. Now though he was wrong in making this attempt, and in venturing to imitate the disciples without receiving a command to do so, yet his boldness was not without success: for the Lord was pleased, in this way also, to throw lustre around his name, as he sometimes does by means of those whose ministry he does not approve as lawful. It is not inconsistent with this to say, that one who was endued with special faith followed a blind impulse, and thus proceeded inconsiderately to work miracles.[8]

Calvin, among his penetrating observations, notes that many details have been providentially left untold so that there is uncertainty in some areas. Yet, the account makes certain items remarkably lucid. The man is reported doing a good deed, casting

---

7. The King James Version reads "us . . . us," but the best Greek texts indicate "you . . . you." However, this does not affect the sense of the passage. Nestle, p. 176.

8. John Calvin, *Commentary on a Harmony of the Evangelists, Matthew, Mark, and Luke,* trans. W. Pringle (3 vols.; Grand Rapids: Eerdmans Publishing Co., 1957), II, 372. This book was translated originally in London in 1584.

out demons, and he is reported to be doing this in the proper way, in Christ's name, not in his own name. Also, as Calvin notes, the man apparently was successful, for the word translated "casting out" is the durative participle, denoting something that continues for a duration, as opposed to a punctiliar occurrence. Calvin, in addition, by saying, "For the Lord was pleased, in this way also, to throw lustre around his name [i.e., around the name of the Lord]," shows that he is of the impression that the man's exorcism of demons glorified the name of Christ.[9] The sacred text does not state or deny this, but it is evident from Calvin's reaction to the text, that there is not textual warrant for assuming that the actions of the man in any way discredited the name of the Lord. Thus, the Bible here reveals a man doing a supernatural deed in the proper way, and the only reason that the disciples forbade him was because he was not of the commissioned twelve.

It is also to be noted that in this case the Lord did not cooperate with the man directly; He did not ask the man to accompany Him, nor did He appear to the people together with him as far as it is known. Christ merely forbade the twelve from stopping him, which they had no authority to do in this case, with the words, "He that is not against us is for us" (Luke 9:50). On these words Lenski observes:

> We should, of course, consider this terse dictum in its connection and not in a mere abstract way. It applies to men like the one under discussion. It does not apply to men who are merely indifferent to Jesus and are thus not actively against him. Such indifference and coldness as a response to Jesus and his revelation (name) would be "against" him and his disciples in a decided way. To be lukewarm and neither hot nor cold is fatal. Thus, not to be against the disciples of Jesus means, indeed, to be for them, at least to some degree. Whoever appreciates Jesus and his name (revelation) enough to drop all opposition to him and to his disciples is, to say the least, on a fair road to becoming his enthusiastic follower.
>
> This shows agreement with the dictum that is voiced in Matt. 12:30 [and also in Luke 11:23 which Dr. Ferm mentions]: "He that is not with me (*meta*) is against me (*kata*)." Both dicta state the same thing, but do so in opposite ways. One states who are for

---

9. *Ibid.*

Jesus, the other who are against him. Both imply that neutrality to him is impossible.[10]

Lenski adequately expresses the import of Christ's saying. Neutrality is impossible! Men are either saved or lost, for Christ or against Christ, heading for heaven or for hell. There is no middle abode! Those who are indifferent, as long as they remain such, have rejected Christ's claims as the Son of God, and their declarations which may enthusiastically acknowledge Him as an extremely good man do not change the picture. Those who deny the historicity of the bodily resurrection and of the virgin birth are not merely liberals, who while intellectually unable to believe, are fine Christians because they claim to be such; but by their wicked unbelief they have shown themselves to be against Christ, and among those who *oppose* Him and His kingdom.

It is seen that since indifference and unbelief are so clearly condemned throughout the New Testament (Matt. 7:26; Luke 14:18; Rev. 3:15,16; John 3:36, 8:24; Matt. 11:21-24, etc.), Lenski does not err in saying, ". . . indifference and coldness as a response to Jesus and his revelation (name) would be 'against' him and his disciples in a decided way. To be lukewarm and neither hot nor cold is fatal."[11] Thus, those indifferent to Christ's claims, though they travel under the label of "liberal," are seen to be in reality "against" Christ, and may properly be said to "oppose" Him. Their opposition takes the form of unbelief, and they are like wolves in sheep's clothing, bleating outwardly of a love for one whom they have rejected inwardly. Despite Ferm's declaration,

> The problem becomes exceedingly complex when one's associations are with nominal Christians, especially when they manifest the Christian graces, yet cannot intellectually accept every tenet of Fundamentalism,[12]

---

10. R. C. H. Lenski, *The Interpretation of St. Luke's Gospel* (Columbus: Wartburg Press, 1946), pp. 550-51.

11. *Ibid.*, p. 550.

12. Ferm, p. 34.

theological liberals who intellectually reject the historic bases of the faith, by their unbelief give the lie to any outward manifestation of what appears to be the Christian graces, and reveal themselves to be those who "oppose" Christ. This is true because unbelief is a sin which involves doing "despite to the Spirit of grace" (Heb. 10:29), and it cannot be discounted on the basis of courtesy, gentle talk, or a river of words about God. It must be remembered that an unbeliever does not wash away his unbelief and show himself to be a true friend of Christ by merely allowing and even aiding a conservative to preach the gospel. This is especially true when the liberal by cooperating with a famous fundamentalist evangelist stands to acquire new members for his church, gain publicly, lessen the enmity which his more conservative parishioners may have for his "intellectual" views by securing the implied approval of the cooperating evangelist, and advance the ecumenical movement by drawing orthodoxy closer to liberalism by the two groups entering upon joint action for a common objective. A wolf does not show himself to be a good fellow by feeding a lamb out of whom he later intends to make a meal.

Matthew 7:22,23 confirms the fact that one can verbalize sweet and great things about God and yet be in the category of "opposers" to Christ. Matthew 7:22,23 says:

> Many will say to me in that day, Lord, Lord, have we not prophesied in thy name? and in thy name have cast out devils? and in thy name done many wonderful works: And I will profess unto them, I never knew you: depart from me, ye that work iniquity.

Conclusions

Thus it is seen with regard to the statement of Dr. Ferm, "If [i.e., since] Jesus accepted the cooperation of any who did not oppose him, . . ." when "oppose" is properly defined in the biblical framework so as to include indifference and unbelief as forms of opposition, then his statement cannot stand.[13] Since his book is defending Billy Graham's cooperation with the liberals, who are

---

13. *Ibid.*, p. 38.

14

unbelievers and heretics, and since he *must* therefore place the unbelieving liberals in the category of those who do not oppose Christ, then it must be concluded that his concept of the word "oppose" is unbiblical, and his proposition is false. This is true because he, Dr. Ferm, has not proved, nor could he prove, that Jesus ever *cooperated* with unsound religious leaders; for "cooperation" used in this sense implies a measure of endorsement which Christ never gave to unbelievers (Matt. 7:21-23). His quoting the incident of the exorcisor of demons being forbidden by the twelve does not prove his case, because there a man is doing a good work in the proper manner without discrediting Christ's name, while in the case of the liberals who have cooperated with Dr. Graham there is clear evidence of their sin of unbelief which brings reproach to Christ's name. It cannot be argued from Christ's defense of one who might have been a believer, who at any rate has not a sin of any weight save possibly rashness of which he can be *proved* guilty, that Christ would also have defended those who are guilty of the sin of unbelief. This is especially true in view of Christ's continual outspoken consternation at this particular sin! There are too many variables to permit Dr. Ferm's analogy to stand.

It is clearly seen that Dr. Ferm's words, "not conducting their mission in precisely the same manner," is completely outside the issue. The issue is whether or not Christ would have Himself joined hands with a liberal unbeliever and appeared together on the same platform with the liberal in one of Christ's own preaching crusades. Dr. Ferm's inclusion of the word "precisely" is probably satire, but the entire sentence is out of place, for no less than the necessity of the purity of the visible Church is at issue. Fundamentalists, in fact have always been the ones famous for hand raisings, mourners' benches, and people coming up the sacred aisle with tearful sobs, so on the issue of method, except as it involves participation with liberals, fundamentalists agree with Dr. Graham's style of conducting evangelistic crusades. Any dispute over method is between the conservative evangelist and the liberal who often dislikes the emotional—conversion aspect of the orthodox evangelist's appeal.

GROUP TWO

ARGUMENTS ADVOCATING COOPERATION WITH THOSE IN SERIOUS DOCTRINAL ERROR

ARGUMENT III

"The Lord Attended the Temple Which Was Dominated by Those Who Erred."

The Argument Advanced by Dr. Ferm

The third of the New Evangelical propositions asserts that the Lord regularly attended the Temple when it was dominated by unprincipled politicians, profiteers, hypocrites, and those who erred doctrinally, and therefore, the evangelist may cooperate with groups having like errors and faults.[1]

The separatist position, it is claimed, would not permit Jesus to enter the Temple at all, not even to cleanse it.[2]

An Examination of Dr. Ferm's Conclusions

The author of *Cooperative Evangelism* declares his beliefs on the significance of Christ's Temple attending by beginning the section with the words, "Jesus himself affords us the best example of cooperation," thus showing that he has concluded this to be a prime evidence for cooperative evangelism.[3] His statement, "Attendance did not imply approval of their conduct or beliefs,"[4] and his quotation of George Adam Smith that, "To him [the Lord] it was the auditorium of the nation, an opportunity of getting at the hearts of men,"[5] indicate that Ferm believes that the Lord's visits gave Him an opportunity to reach the nation which He would not otherwise have had, and that by them the Lord did not

---

1. *Ibid.*, pp. 36-37.
2. *Ibid.*
3. *Ibid.*
4. *Ibid.*
5. *Ibid.*, p. 37, quoting George Adam Smith, Jerusalem, II, 524.

imply approval of the errors present in the hearts and practices of the Temple's so-called "Leaders."

Now, to orientate Dr. Ferm's conclusions, Dr. Ferm's purpose of writing is to defend a conservative evangelist's, Billy Graham's, method of cooperating with liberals, by showing that the Lord cooperated with errorists by preaching in a place dominated by them. It is argued that, since by doing this the Lord obtained a wider hearing *while not implying approval of the errors or of the errorists*, Billy Graham *by doing the same thing* is obtaining a wider hearing while not giving approval to the liberals or their doctrinal unbelief.

Dr. Ferm also states somewhat sarcastically, "Had Jesus acted upon the general principle of separation as interpreted by the present-day separatists, he would not have visited the Temple, *not even to cleanse it.*"[6] (Italics mine)

The Writer's Critique

Since the comparison is drawn between the New Evangelical method in general and the Lord's visitation of the Temple, it is profitable to note the tenor of the Lord's Temple visits, the tenor of his sayings about the Temple, and the tenor of His dealings with the leaders who abided in the Temple. The visits cited on the table on the next page, Table 1, are all those noted as Temple visits in A. T. Robertson's harmony of the Gospels,[7] and while it is sometimes difficult to determine on other occasions if Christ was or was not in the Temple, those tabulated certainly give a sufficient picture of the case.

TABLE 1

OUR LORD'S TEMPLE VISITS WHICH ARE DESCRIBED AT SOME LENGTH IN SCRIPTURES

1. a. Occasion: His presentation to the Lord at infancy.
   b. Scripture: Luke 2:22-38.
   c. Tenor : Simeon and Anna pay homage to the infant Messiah.

---

6. *Ibid.*

7. A. T. Robinson, *A Harmony of the Gospels for Students of the Life of Christ* (New York: Harper & Brothers, 1922), secs. 13, 18, 31, 96, 98, 99, 111, 129, 132-38.

2. a. Occasion: Annual Jerusalem visit.
   b. Scripture: Luke 2:41-50.
   c. Tenor : Christ at twelve discusses with the Doctors. He calls the Temple his "Father's house."

3. a. Occasion: Passover visit.
   b. Scripture: John 2:13-22.
   c. Tenor : Christ cleanses the Temple first time. Controversy!

4. a. Occasion: Christ teaches the people during the Feast of Tabernacles.
   b. Scripture: John 7:11-52.
   c. Tenor : Christ defends his healing on the sabbath, and the rulers attempt to have him arrested. Controversy!

5. a. Occasion: Teaching in the treasury of the Temple after the Feast of the Tabernacles.
   b. Scripture: John 8:12-20.
   c. Tenor : Jesus tells the Pharisees that they do not know the Father. Controversy!

6. a. Occasion: Teaching in the Temple, perhaps during the same visit as on the occasion of John 8:12-20.
   b. Scripture: John ·8:21-59.
   c. Tenor : The Jews attempt to stone Jesus. Controversy!

7. a. Occasion: The Jews come to Jesus in the Temple at the Feast.
   b. Scripture: John 10:22-39.
   c. Tenor : The Jews attempt to stone him. Controversy!

8. a. Occasion: Jesus enters the Temple on Monday of the Passion Week.
   b. Scripture: Mark 11:15-18; Matthew 21:12-13; Luke 19:45-46.
   c. Tenor : Christ cleanses the Temple the second time. Controversy!

9. a. Occasion: The remainder of Christ's Passion Week Temple appearances; chiefly and perhaps entirely on Tuesday.
   b. Scripture: Luke 19:47-48; Matthew 21:22-23; 39 and the parallel passages to these verses in Matthew's Gospel.
   c. Tenor : Continuous controversy with the Jewish leaders.

10. a. Occasion: Christ sitting over against the treasury notices the widow's mite.
    b. Scripture: Mark 12:41-44; Luke 21:1-4.
    c. Tenor : A teaching on giving is made to his disciples which sheds no real light on Christ's relations to the Temple or its leaders.

Examining Christ's visits to the Temple, His infancy and regular boyhood visits combined with His regular attendance at feast days during His ministry, one cannot help but see that the Temple was certainly rightfully God's house in the eyes of Christ. However, on the basis of the information indicated in Table 1, it is seen that the Lord's words in Matthew 21:13 give the complete picture, declaring, "It is written, My house shall be called the house of prayer; but ye have made it a den of thieves." His open declaration of the error which He beheld in the Temple, mirrored in His words, "But ye have made it a den of thieves" (Matt. 21:13), formed a regular part of his Temple visits during His ministry. He rebuked the error of the leaders, as well as that of the people, whenever and wherever He found it in the Temple, and in no case did any of His Temple visitations give the people the impression that He was cooperating with the Pharisees, chief priests, or other rulers of the Temple. This will be seen even more clearly in the examination of His attitude and the words to the so-called leaders of the Temple.

Along with Christ's visits to the Temple, among His many comments with regard to it, the following should be noted: (1) In Matthew 17:24-27 Christ pays the stater found miraculously in the fish's mouth as His payment of the Temple tax saying, "Lest we cause them to stumble, . . ." Thus while declaring Himself to be the Son of God and therefore not having to pay the tax to His own Father, He pays it in order not to place a stumbling block in front of the people, who might look upon refusal to pay as dis-respect and indifference to Jehovah of the Temple. (2) In Matthew 23:17 Christ asks, "Ye fools and blind: for whether is greater, the gold, or the temple that sanctifieth the gold?" Here Christ acknowledges that the Temple, despite the corruption of the leaders who inhabit it, has a sanctifying power. Other comments of Christ which involve the Temple such as its future destruction, Matthew 24:2, are in the realm of eschatology and do not significantly display Christ's attitude toward it.

Besides Jesus' visitations to the Temple, and His comments on it, there is to be considered His general attitude and relationship with the leaders who ruled the sacred house. The Chief Priests, the Pharisees, the Sadducees, the Scribes, the Elders, and the moneychangers and sellers of animals were the ones who controlled the Temple, and the New Testament reveals only hostility and disapproval on the part of Jesus toward each and every one of these overlapping groups. Christ challenged the Chief Priests and the Elders before the people for their unbelief in the authority of John the Baptist, and openly declared to them that, "The publicans and harlots go into the Kingdom of God before you" (Matt. 21:31; 21:23-46). In Matthew 23:13-26, in an unparalleled display of righteous indignation, Christ refers to the Scribes and Pharisees as "hypocrites," "fools," "blind," "whited sepulchres," "serpents," "generation of vipers," and questions them, "How can ye escape the damnation of hell?" In Matthew 16:6 Christ warns, "Take heed and beware of the leaven of the Pharisees and of the Sadducees," and in Mark 8:15 He adds the command to beware also of "the leaven of Herod [i.e., of the Herodians]." As for the moneychangers and sellers of animals in the sacred house, Christ "made a scourge of small cords, . . . drove them all out of the temple, . . . and poured out the changer's money, and overthrew the tables" (John 2:15): and this He did twice (John 2:13-22 and 21:12-13; Mark 11:15-18; Luke 19:45, 46).

Thus it is seen that one of the dominant characteristics, if not the dominant characteristic, of the Lord's Temple visitations which occurred after His boyhood and during His ministry, was the Lord's continual struggle with the leaders of Jewry. He rebuked them freely and openly before the people, so that everyone knew that there was enmity between the Lord and the Pharisees and other Temple dominants, and so that there was never even a moment when any of the action or words of the Lord could be construed as His giving approval to their wicked practices, unbelief, or persons. Herein lies the reason for the lack of confusion: the Lord's preaching the whole counsel of God and rebuking sin and sinners wherever He found it, and especially in the leaders who frequented the Temple! With these facts in mind, it cannot be successfully defended that the Lord "cooperated with the ruling parties of the Temple in any sense of "giving approval" to their erroneous practices, doctrines, or unbelief. In fact, in view of the New Testament's account of the continual increasing mutual antagonism and hostility between Christ and the leaders of Jewry, it is seen that the Temple was merely the common sacred arena in which a "holy war" was fought, and it cannot be honestly said that Jesus "cooperated" with the Temple leaders at all. Therefore, Dr. Ferm's statement concerning Christ that, "Attendance did not imply approval of their [the Temple leaders'] conduct or beliefs," is true *because* Christ's banner always flew high and He continually rebuked the sins of the leaders.[8] While He also proclaimed His message of life, He deliberately made it impossible for anyone to misinterpret His Temple attendance as any sign of favor upon the errors in life or doctrine of the wicked rulers.

On the Lord's attitude toward Jewry's leaders, Dr. Cornelius Van Til makes the following penetrating observation:

> Ferm's appeal to Jesus' earthly ministry for support of cooperative evangelism is singularly unfortunate. The only real parallel between the situation of our day and that of Jesus pertains to the religious leaders of the time. However much they disagreed among themselves on other matters they agreed on the idea of salvation by works or character. And they ruled in the one organization on earth raised up for the dissemination of the idea of salvation by grace. So, as they did not invite Jesus to cooperate in preaching their gospel with them so Jesus did not invite them to preach his gospel with them. Jesus *made provision for their removal* from their position of leadership among the people. The establishment of his kingdom was predicted on the destruction of theirs. Their house would be left desolate to them. "Woe unto you, scribes and Pharisees, hypocrites! for ye compass sea and land to make one proselyte, and when he is made, ye make him twofold more the child of hell than yourselves" (Matt. 23:15).[9]

Dr. Ferm's satirical remark, "Had Jesus acted upon the general principle of separation as interpreted by the present-day separatist, he would not have visited the Temple, not even to cleanse it,"[10] reflects a complete misapprehension of the principle of separation. The very point to be understood is the fact that separatists do approve of Jesus' visitation to the Temple *because* of the fact that He did cleanse it! What separatists would not have approved of, which the Lord by nature would never have done, would have been the Lord's asking one of the

---

8. Ferm, p. 36.

9. Cornelius Van Til, *The New Evangelicalism* (Philadelphia: Westminster Theological Seminary, 1962) Mimeographed, pp. 26-27.

10. Ferm, p. 37.

Sadducees who did not believe in the resurrection (Matt. 22:23) to lead in a word of prayer before He, the Lord, began to teach in the Temple. Instead of that, the Lord condemned the Sadducean error with the words, "Ye do err, not knowing the scriptures, nor the power of God" (Matt. 22:29). The separatists would have objected if the Lord had asked one of the Pharisees, who erred by making the Law of God an instrument of spiritless formalism and works, to be chairman of the committee in charge of dealing with those who desire to make a decision. The Lord did not do this, however, for He could not congratulate unrighteousness even if it cost Him publicity, popularity, and opportunity to preach the Word. Instead the Lord called the Pharisee a "child of hell" (Matt. 23:15) and warned the lambs against him. The separatists would have cried out if the Lord, who could not have done such, had turned over new converts to some of the churches of the chief priests. Instead the Lord placed such a value on His little ones that He said, "It were better for him that a millstone were hanged about his neck, and he cast into the sea, than he should offend one of these little ones" (Luke 17:2); and Christ declared plainly to the chief priests that, "The publicans and harlots go into the Kingdom of God before you" (Matt. 21:31). Thus the separatists do not object per se to a cooperative evangelist's entrance into a particular church or meeting hall which contains modernists in it. They object to the approval given to the modernists and to modernism by the conservative's calling upon the modernist to lead in prayer, head up committees, take part in counseling those making a decision, and the conservative's directing converts into known liberal churches, in addition to the conservative's complete silence on the question of modernism. This type of action gives a real note of approval to the liberals, it makes liberalism seem to be only a mere theological variant among intellectuals instead of the wicked sin and heresy that it is. This confuses the public, especially God's children who have confidence in the conservative evangelist. It harms the new converts which Jesus loves, it violates Christ's commands to beware of false prophets (Matt. 7:15), and it displays a friendliness to unbelief quite the opposite of Jesus' continual hatred and vexation at it.

22

Conclusions

Thus the analogy between our Lord's attendance in the Temple and cooperation with known liberals is seen to be completely invalid. This is because the Lord continually rebuked the sins of the leaders of the Temple and warned the people against them, while New Evangelicals deal with the modernists as friends, as righteous men, and as proper stewards of the souls of others, without rebuking their sin of unbelief and false shepherding. This sinful befriending and approving of the wicked on the grounds of securing additional opportunity to preach the Gospel is using the ends to justify the means, which is an evil practice. Thus, this third argument is based upon a false analogy, and must be understood to be completely invalid.

ARGUMENT IV

"The Lord Attended the Synagogue Which Was Dominated by Those Who Erred"

The Argument Advanced by Dr. Ferm

The fourth proposition of the non-separatists maintains that the Lord regularly entered and participated in the worship of the synagogue when many rulers of the synagogues expected only an earthly messianic kingdom and an immediate temporal restoration of Israel by the Messiah. Therefore, it is felt that the evangelist can likewise cooperate with groups which are doctrinally unsound.[1]

It is further put forward that the separatist position would accuse Christ of compromise because of His synagogue attendance and participation in the service of the Nazarene Synagogue when He read and commented on the Scriptures in that place (Luke 4:16-31).[2]

An Examination of Dr. Ferm's Conclusions

Dr. Ferm on behalf of New Evangelicalism has concluded that since doctrinal and other errors did not keep the Lord from participating in the worship of the synagogues and from teaching in them, the doctrinal errors prevalent today in so many of the leaders and pastors of the larger denominations should not keep the conservative evangelist from cooperating with them in his imperative to preach the Gospel. Here, as always, it must be kept in mind that Dr. Ferm's purpose is to justify Billy Graham's cooperating with liberals as well as with conservatives. Every analysis of Dr. Ferm's conclusions must take this primary aim into consideration in order to see what he is attempting to prove and in order to see the true nature of his analogies. In this case, he is equating the errors of the synagogue with the errors of today's liberals, and he is equating the Lord's teaching in the synagogues

---

1. *Ibid.,* pp. 37-38.

2. *Ibid.*

with Billy Graham's cooperating with known modernists in bringing to the public a conservative message without warnings against liberal and neo-orthodox heresies and heretics.

Dr. Ferm's remark, "Present-day separatists would most certainly have pointed an accusing finger at him [the Lord] for what they might consider compromise [i.e., the Lord's teaching in the synagogues]," shows that he feels that separatists are legalistically condemning Dr. Graham for merely entering certain doors, rather than primarily condemning his conduct of friendliness and approval to modernists inside of those doors.[3]

The Writer's Critique

Here, just as in the case of the Lord's visits to the Temple, it will be profitable to note some of the details of Christ's synagogue attendance, and its general tenor with respect to His conduct in the synagogues and His dealings with the synagogue leaders and worshipers.

The New Testament makes it abundantly clear that Christ made it a regular practice to teach in the synagogues of the region in which he was ministering. Matthew 4:23 declares, "And Jesus went about all Galilee, teaching in their synagogues, and preaching the gospel of the kingdom, . . ." Other verses which indicate His general practice of teaching in the synagogues would be, Matthew 9:35; Mark 1:39; Luke 4:15,44; and John 18:20.

A. T. Robinson's harmony of the gospel accounts indicates as synagogue visits those shown on the following table, Table 2.[4] Again, as in the case of the Temple, it must be noted that other sayings and occurrences related in the gospels might have taken place in the synagogues but cannot be so identified because the Scriptures do not identify the location of their genesis. The occasion of the visit, the scriptural reference, and the tenor of the encounter will be noted in each case on the table located on the following page.

---

3. *Ibid.*, p. 37.

4. Robertson, secs. 39, 42, 51, 69, 76, and 110.

TABLE 2

OUR LORD'S SYNAGOGUE VISITS WHICH ARE DESCRIBED AT SOME LENGTH IN THE SCRIPTURES

1. a. Occasion: Christ enters the Nazareth synagogue on the sabbath.
   b. Scripture: Luke 4:16-31.
   c. Tenor : Christ reads; the people are skeptical; Christ upbraids them; the people attempt to kill Christ.

2. a. Occasion: Christ teaches in the Capernaum synagogue on the sabbath.
   b. Scripture: Mark 1:21-28; Luke 4:31-37.
   c. Tenor : Christ teaches; casts out a demon; the people are amazed.

3. a. Occasion: Christ enters a Galilean synagogue on the sabbath.
   b. Scripture: Mark 3:1-6; Matthew 12:9-14; Luke 6:6-11.
   c. Tenor : The Pharisees watch to accuse him of healing on the sabbath; Jesus, angered at them, heals a man; the Pharisees go out and counsel how to kill Christ.

4. a. Occasion: Christ teaches in the Nazareth synagogue on the sabbath.
   b. Scripture: Mark 6:1-6; Matthew 13:54-58.
   c. Tenor : Jesus teaches; the people were astonished and offended at him; he could do no mighty work there because of their unbelief.

5. a. Occasion: A crowd from among the five thousand whom Christ fed seek Jesus because he had fed their bodies, and they find him on the other side of the Sea of Tiberias on the day following in the synagogue at Capernaum.
   b. Scripture: John 6:22-71.
   c. Tenor : The crowd finds Christ in the synagogue; he rebukes their carnality and reveals himself as the true bread from heaven, and not a political messiah; the crowd forsakes him upon learning this.

6. a. Occasion: Christ teaches in a Judean synagogue on the sabbath.
   b. Scripture: Luke 13:10-21.
   c. Tenor : Christ heals a woman on the sabbath; the ruler of the synagogue publicly rebukes this practice; Christ calls the objectors "Hypocrites," and by his words he shames his adversaries and causes his followers to rejoice.

Matthew 9:18-26, Mark 5:22-43, and Luke 8:41-56 also give an extended account of an additional occasion besides the one mentioned in Luke 13:10-21 in which the Lord dealt with another Ruler of the Synagogue. This man whose name was Jairus, who possessed a measure of faith, had his daughter raised from the dead.

Omitting Christ's words on the persecutions which awaited His disciples in the future from the synagogues, Christ often also decried the hypocrites who loved the pre-eminence in the synagogues (Matt. 6:2,5; 23:6; Mark 12:39; Luke 11:43; and 20:46). The only other item of note which directly mentions the synagogue or its rulers is found in the verses John 9:22 and 12:42,43. Both of these passages reveal the fact that the antagonism between Christ and those who had the authority over certain of the synagogues had become so acute that the Pharisees had decided to "put out of the synagogue" any who confessed Christ, even if he should be a "chief Ruler" (John 12:42). A. T. Robertson places in the Later Judean Ministry the saying of John 9:22 which tells of this agreement to put out of the synagogue any who confessed Christ, and he places in the Last Public Ministry in Jerusalem the similar verse of John 12:42; thus showing that in the latter portion of the Lord's earthly ministry if not earlier, many rulers of the synagogues had only hatred for Christ.[5]

Thus it is observed that Christ habitually taught on the sabbath in the synagogue of the region that He was ministering in at the time. During these visitations He cast out demons, healed, and revealed Himself. His actions and words caused the reactions of unbelief and hatred in those who were not His own. The healing and casting out of demons on the sabbath especially incurred the wrath of the hypocritical Pharisees who interpreted the sabbath with a deadening letterism which was foreign to the true intent of the sabbath law. The antagonism between Christ and those Pharisees who had authority over the synagogues continually grew more bitter and acrimonious. By the Later Judean Ministry, anyone who confessed Jesus as the Christ was put out of the synagogue even if he was a person of authority himself, thus intimidating the fearful. The visits of Christ into the synagogues were characterized by a continually heightening controversy which time after time saw Christ publicly rebuking those who objected to Himself and to His healing. Christ who could have easily made appointments with the afflicted to heal them either on the day

5. *Ibid.*, secs. 100 and 130.

before or the day after the sabbath in order to avoid offending the Pharisees and in order to placate those synagogue rulers who were hostile, is seen in Matthew 12:9-14 and Luke 13:10-21 healing on the sabbath in the very presence of those who despised Him for this practice. It is no wonder that out of the six synagogue visits which are treated in detail in the Bible, enumerated on Table 2, one ends with an attempt to kill Christ, another ends with the Pharisees seeking counsel on how to kill Him, a third concludes with the crowd forsaking Him, a fourth with Christ after a controversy doing no mighty work there because of their unbelief, and a fifth climaxes with Christ calling "hypocrites" those who were offended by His having healed on the seventh day. Out of the six, only on the visit to the Capernaum synagogue which according to Robertson's harmony would have taken place at the very beginning of Christ's coming there to dwell, early in His public ministry, was a reaction recorded of amazement and astonishment (Mark 1:22,27; Luke 4:32), without mention of any actual controversy.[6]

Thus, the situation between the Lord and the synagogues could be summed up with the words: Christ habitually during His ministry taught in the synagogues on the sabbath, and while He drew many of His own to Himself, for the most part He fought a continuing and heightening acrimonious battle with the authorities in which He unceasingly challenged and rebuked their unbelief in Himself and their hypcritical bitterness at His healing on the seventh day. This battle constantly increased their hatred of Him until at last the Pharisees resolved not only to put anyone out of the synagogue who confessed Him, but also to kill Christ Himself.

With these findings as a result of an examination of the biblical accounts, Dr. Ferm's analogy and application can be properly critiqued. As to Dr. Ferm's first analogy which equates the errors of the synagogue with the errors of liberalism, one can say that both contained errors, while it is a more complex task to evaluate their comparative severity. The synagogues accepted the Old Testament as the Word of God which the liberals do not,

---

6. *Ibid.*, sec. 42 and pp. 32-34 and xvii.

which tends to bend the scale of blackness in the modernist's direction. Although the synagogue leaders in those days erred too often in making theirs an ethical rather than a redemptive religion, *until after* Christ appeared and they rejected Him, they were not sinning against a particle of the light which the liberals of today have. The liberals of today, despite their pious words which unbelievers too can utter (Matt. 7:15,22,23) and despite whatever label they travel under, have rejected the Christ of the Scriptures who is one true savior, and taken to themselves another Christ who is not "another" (*allos*—another of the same kind) but "another" (*heteros*—another of a different kind).[7]

Although both the majority of the synagogue authorities and the liberals are guilty of unbelief and rejection of Christ in the face of great light, the one having the Savior and His miracles in person and the other having the completion of the written revelation in the New Testament, yet there is a notable difference as to *the time* of the climax of their sin. In the case of the synagogue authorities since *the visitation* of them by Christ constituted the great light against which they sinned, before He entered the synagogues they were not guilty of sinning in the face of such great light. When Christ visited them, as He entered, they had not yet sinned against the fullness of their light. Their sin against the great light could only be noted as final at the conclusion of the Lord's synagogue visits. This also was the case of the synagogues which Paul visited outside of Israel. At the conclusion of these visits by Christ and Paul the synagogues stood condemned as rejecting great light and were in turn rejected by the Church. *Thus*, the sin of the synagogue rulers *before* Christ visited them, was not a sin against as much light as the sin of the liberals *before* Dr. Graham entered their dwelling. This is because the liberals had sinned against great light *before* their visitation while the synagogue rulers sinned against great light only *during* their visitation *and not before it*. Thus the analogy of Dr. Ferm in comparing the sins of the two camps of different ages *before their visitation* by Christ or the evangelist is not in fact completely proper for the

---

7. Cf. Gal. 1:6-7.

liberals are guilty of greater sin *at that stage* because they had rejected the Savior in the face of the greater illumination, and because they reject the written Word which the synagogues did at least receive however they might have misinterpreted it.

As to Dr. Ferm's second analogy which equates the conduct of the Lord in this area with the conduct of the modern cooperative evangelist, without the necessity of such an abstruse analysis which the first comparison was subjected to, it is seen that it too cannot stand. It cannot stand because the attitude and mood of the Lord in dealing with the errorists which He found in the synagogues has been shown to be one of constant uncompromising rebuke in which He brought the issues out before the public and warned the people. His doing this cost Him opportunity to proclaim His message, opportunity to teach the people, and eventually humanly speaking it cost Him His life. It divided the people, and centered a continuous and bitterly growing controversy around Him. Its acrimoniousness was so intense and fierce that only His blood could satiate the appetites of those whom He had publicly dubbed as "hypocrites." This is what the scriptures reveal concerning the Lord's synagogue participation.

The attitude and mood of cooperative evangelism has been one of cooperation, handshaking, trust, conciliation, fellowship, and approval. This has been manifested by the evangelist's kind words, permitting of the liberals to assume such positions of esteem as prayer leaders, counselors, and sponsors, and by the evangelists trusting the care of the babes in Christ into the hands of those who question the inerrancy of the Scriptures.

Dr. Ferm's words, "Present-day separatists would most certainly have pointed an accusing finger at him [the Lord] for what they might consider compromise [i.e., for entering the synagogues],"[8] are seen to be unfounded because the separatists do not object to a conservative's entering a house filled with error and sin as long as the conservative along with his Gospel message somewhere makes it clear that in God's book the error and sin that is in the particular house is wicked and sinful. However, the

---

8. Ferm, p. 37.

30

separatist does point the accusing finger at a conservative who enters a temple of idols and asks one of the Baal priests to lead in prayer, preaches a good gospel message and denounces sin in general, poses with his arm about the leader of the temple, directs the new converts to a Baal priestess with the words that the Holy Spirit will look after His own (which He will, *despite* the disobedience of the conservative in question), and leaves saying that the Baal gang really believes a lot of things similar to our own faith and are a "swell bunch" when one gets to really know them. This type of service which makes God's flock wonder if the liberals are really sinful after all, disobeys the spirit of 2 Corinthians 6:14-7:1, as well as the spirit of a holy Jehovah who hates sin.

Conclusions

Dr. Ferm has advanced two analogies within the proposition under discussion. In the first he equated the sin of the synagogue authorities before Christ's entrance to the sin of the present day liberals before the entrance of the orthodox evangelist. This analogy has been shown not to be quite proper for the liberals had sinned under great light *before* the entrance of the cooperative evangelist, while the synagogue rulers had not sinned under equally great light before the entrance of Christ—for as Christ's entrance provided their great light, they sinned *in its presence* only *during* His visitation and not before it. Thus the sin of the liberals before the entrance of the evangelist is greater than the sin of the synagogue authorities before the entrance of Christ, because at this stage the former had received the greater illumination. Also, the synagogues, although they misinterpreted it often, received the written Word of God which the liberals do not.

The second analogy of Dr. Ferm within this fourth proposition, however, is where the major fallacy lies, for it has been Biblically shown that the Lord's fixed attitude against the unbelievers and the other errorists was one of righteous indignation, vexation, hostility, and rebuke; while it has been seen that the fixed attitude of cooperative evangelism toward the unbelieving modernists is one of conciliation, cooperation, fellowship, and approval.

With the questioning of the validity of Dr. Ferm's first analogy, and with the complete demise of his second, it is seen that the fourth argument, which has its foundations upon these two comparisons, cannot be considered as reliable and therefore must be abandoned.

ARGUMENT V

"The Lord Engaged in Religious Contact and Conversation with Religious Rejects"

The Argument Advanced by Dr. Ferm

The fifth proposal which is advanced by the Cooperative Evangelists claims that, "Against the risk of being misunderstood by the legalists, Christ engaged in contact and conversation with the religious rejects,"[1] and therefore, the evangelist of today may cooperate with the religious rejects in the work of proclaiming the Gospel in order to win many who are in spiritual need.

In this line of thought, Dr. Ferm boldly affirms, "If the contacts of Jesus with the Temple and synagogue are not enough to satisfy the critics, there still remain the many instances of his contacts with people of questionable as well as impeccable character and conduct."[2] He then substantiates this declaration with such scriptures as Luke 15:1,2, "All the publicans and sinners were drawing near unto him to hear him. And both the Pharisees and the Scribes murmured, saying, This man receiveth sinners, and eateth with them;" and Matthew 9:12, "They that are whole have no need of a physician, but they that are sick." Finally he concludes, *"There appears to be no way that the cooperative policy of Billy Graham can be shown to be inconsistent with that established by the conduct of Christ."*[3]

An Examination of Dr. Ferm's Conclusions

As Dr. Graham has never been called into question for preaching *to* crowds of sinners but only for cooperating with liberal leaders, Dr. Graham's cooperation with liberals must be the item compared to Christ's cooperation with some group. Since the Pharisees are mentioned by Dr. Ferm as having criticized the

---

1. *Ibid.*, p. 39.
2. *Ibid.*
3. *Ibid.*

Lord's cooperative policy, they could not be the sinners with whom the Lord cooperated. The only other group in this case which is left for the Lord to have cooperated with is the Publicans and sinners. Thus, Dr. Ferm's words indicate that he is of the opinion that Dr. Graham's conduct toward today's liberal leaders is analogous to Christ's behavior toward the Publicans and sinners; and that the nature of Christ's conduct toward them was one of cooperation! This may at first seem startling, but this is exactly what this New Evangelical spokesman is maintaining!

The implication of Dr. Ferm's words clearly shows that he deems the Pharisee's criticizing of Christ's contacts with the Publicans as comparable with the fundamentalist's censuring of Dr. Graham for cooperating with sinners, notably the liberal theological leaders. This again shows that in Dr. Ferm's mind the Publicans and sinners are analogous to the liberal religious leaders and pastors of today.

The Writer's Critique

The first thing to be noted is the nature of Christ's conduct with each of the two groups of sinners, the Publicans and sinners on the one hand and the Pharisees and other religious dominants on the other.

The Publicans were sinners as other lost men were, but because their office gave them unique opportunity to despoil their neighbors, they became a despicable byword to the people symbolizing greed and avarice. Christ in Matthew 18:17 commands His people that anyone who refuses to hear the Church is to be treated by the Church as "a heathen and a publican," thus showing that He too saw the corruption in the Publicans. However, His calling of Matthew, a Publican, to be a disciple (Matt. 9:9), His parable of the Pharisee and the Publican (Luke 18:9-14), and His declaring, "Verily I say unto you, That the publicans and the harlots go into the kingdom of God before you [the chief priests, elders, and Pharisees]" (Matt. 21:13), indicate that Christ saw in this group needy sinners who could, and often did, repent, believe, and become saved. For this cause the Lord went among them, saying, when the Pharisees accused Him of eating with Publicans and sinners, "They that be whole need not a physician but they that are sick" (Matt. 9:12). He looked upon them as sick with sin, and His relation to them was that of a physician who cured all who would yield to His treatment. He never cooperated with the Publicans, harlots, or other sinners in the work of the proclamation of God's tidings, except as in the case of Matthew, after they had been converted and had left the class of "sinners" and entered the realm of "disciples."

As has been seen in the previous sections of this thesis, Christ's conduct with unconverted Pharisees and religious authorities was the very opposite of cooperative. Between them and Christ there was only continual rebuke, growing conflict, acrimonious public debate, and finally, the leaders of Israel desired nothing less than Christ's death (Matt. 12:14). To them, their false leading of the people, and their self-righteousness the Lord declared, "Woe unto you, scribes and Pharisees, hypocrites! for ye compass sea and land to make one proselyte, and when he is made, ye make him twofold more the child of hell than yourselves" (Matt. 23:15). His opinion of the chances of the self-righteous leaders being converted as compared to the chances of the immoral sinners, is summed up in his words to the leaders, saying, "Verily I say unto you, That the publicans and harlots go into the kingdom of God before you" (Matt. 21:31).

As for Dr. Ferm's comparisons, the conservative cooperative evangelist likewise deals with two primary groups of sinners germane to the present discussion, the lost who sit in the pews and the unbelievers who sit on the platform.[4] The sinners in the pews should be most properly compared to the Publicans and sinners to whom Christ went as a physician to the sick. These pew inhabitants are acknowledged by the evangelist as sick and he does not ask them to help in the spreading of the Gospel until they are well. The liberal unbelievers on the platform as the false religious leaders and the self-righteous who reject the Christ of the Scriptures, should be compared with the Pharisees who also were

---

4. Of course, conservatives also cooperate with the evangelist, and sit on the platform, but that is not the subject at issue.

false self-righteous religious authorities who rejected Christ. Although there are grave differences in the two, the liberals rejecting the validity and inerrancy of the written Word and the Pharisees representing a pre-Christ orthodoxy of deadening formalism, yet the point of analogy is the fact that they are both false religious leaders who reject the true Christ, who are unsaved, and who are blind leaders of the blind.

Even if in some cases certain separatists should have fallen into the Pharisaical error of hyper-legalism, yet in their fundamental adherence to faith in the risen Christ as the only way of salvation they are true lights, and not false leaders who reject the true Savior. However, in actuality here the fundamentalists are those who echo Paul in 2 Corinthians 6:14-7:1, and who echo Jehu's words to Jehosaphat in 2 Chronicles 19:2, "Shouldest thou help the ungodly, and love them that hate the LORD? therefore is wrath upon thee from before the LORD." They are not hyper-legalists, but Christians who are declaring a biblical truth, and therefore, they are improperly compared by Dr. Ferm's implication to the Pharisees!

Thus the analogies of Dr. Ferm are not only highly questionable as to their aptness, but the writer of this thesis believes that they are here invalid completely. The Lord's conduct toward Publicans and sinners cannot properly be compared to Dr. Graham's conduct toward the liberal leaders; but the Lord's conduct toward the Pharisees and other false leaders ought to be the measure of Dr. Graham's conduct to the false modernists of today.

However, regardless of the accuracy of Dr. Ferm's analogies of the groups, on the evaluation of the analogy of the conduct between Chirst and Dr. Graham which Dr. Ferm draws, it is seen that Dr. Graham's conduct is *not* analogous to *either* Christ's behavior to the Publicans *or* to the Pharisees! This is because Dr. Graham's behavior toward the liberal leaders is one of cooperation, trust, fellowship, and approval as religious authorities who are well and whole, while Christ treated the Publicans and sinners as sick, in need of repentance, and capable of being saved only if they repented and believed. In neither case did Christ cooperate with either group in order to get additional opportunity or in order to obtain additional aid; He only cooperated with individuals from either group who by their repentance and faith had severed their former allegiance. Truly Dr. Ferm is correct when he says that, "Christ engaged in contact and conversation with the religious rejects,"[5] but this was to cure them as sick people and not to get their help. Thus it is that Dr. Graham is not criticized for "contact and conversation with the religious rejects," but for placing in positions of trust and leadership not the "religious rejects" but the "blind leaders," and for his contact and conversation with them not as ill people, but as whole physicians.

Conclusions

It has been seen that Dr. Ferm's analogy between Christ's "contact and conversation with the religious rejects" and cooperative evangelism's cooperation with modernists in bringing to the public the Word of God, is a false analogy on two points.[6] It has been shown that Christ dealt with the religious rejects as ill people who needed a physician while cooperative evangelism deals with them as whole people capable of helping to cure others, thus negating the point of comparison. It has also been shown that Dr. Ferm makes the liberal leaders of today analogous to the Publicans and sinners, and that this analogy cannot be sustained because the liberals primarily are false leaders who would better be compared to the false leaders of Christ's time, while the Publicans and sinners being sick sinners who occupy no position of leadership would better be compared to the unsaved sinners who sit in the pews. Thus, the fifth argument has been shown to be based on analogies that cannot truly be substantiated, and therefore, it must be regarded as invalid.

---

5. Ferm, p. 39.
6. *Ibid.*

37

GROUP THREE

ARGUMENTS ADVOCATING THAT THE EMPHASIS OF THE LORD'S MINISTRY FAVORS COOPERATIVE EVANGELISM

ARGUMENT VI

"Judge Not, that Ye Be Not Judged"

The Argument Advanced by Dr. Ferm

The sixth New Evangelical contention is that the Lord specifically has *forbidden* us against sitting in judgment against other Christians. In addition to this it is said that, "In city-wide meetings . . . it would be *impossible* [italics mine] to set up a local committee that would agree on which churches are worthy and which are not"; and the judging of human associations to whom the one who makes a decision will be directed is *not here necessary* since the "Holy Spirit must be trusted to perfect the work which he has begun."[1]

Dr. Ferm feels that the issue resides "in the realm of Christian ethics."[2] He boldly asserts that,

> Any minister or church that willingly enters into a cooperative effort, where the Gospel is to be preached without restrictions of any kind, is certainly deserving of having converts who so desire to join in the fellowship of that particular church. If later any are led astray, or spiritually starved, the responsibility rests squarely on those churches, not the evangelist. To take any other course is to sit in judgment on other Christians, something against which our Lord specifically warns us.[3]

---

1. *Ibid.*, p. 19.
2. *Ibid.*
3. *Ibid.*

An Examination of Dr. Ferm's Conclusions

Dr. Ferm has concluded that the Lord has specifically forbidden us to sit in judgment of another Christian's doctrinal soundness, but since he does not state his Scriptural grounds for this, it will be impossible to state positively upon what verse or verses he has arrived at his conclusion; however, Matthew 7:1, "Judge not, that ye be not judged," and its immediate context is most likely the bulwark upon which his case rests. This verse during recent years has been the one cast into the teeth of countless separatists as the verse which condemns them for denouncing the modernists for their unbelief.

Despite Dr. Ferm's remark concerning proof texts used by the separatists, in which he declares, "It is evident that such verses are not to be found in great abundance, for the same few are used repeatedly,"[4] it is realized by the writer of this study that if this single text, or any single text, stands upon a sound textual basis and teaches a doctrine, admonition, or fact clearly and plainly in the light of sound historical grammatical and contextual exegetical interpretation, then that teaching must stand regardless if no other verse in the Bible reiterates its precise emphasis.

Dr. Ferm's words, ". . . to sit in judgment on *other Christians* [italics mine]," would indicate that he has concluded the known and outspoken liberals, who are the target of the judging of which he speaks, to be in the company of those called "Christians."[5] Their being such in name cannot be denied, but their unbelief in the essential historic doctrines would remove them from the category of "other," i.e., fellow, "Christians," and more accurately place them in an ethical society which, while rejecting the historic truths of Scripture, claims to accept many of its moral admonitions.

Dr. Ferm has also obviously concluded that a local committee cannot possibly decide which churches desiring to participate in a large crusade are sound and which are unsound; and that the evangelist can with good conscience send those who have come

---

4. *Ibid.*, p. 44.
5. *Ibid.*, p. 19.

39

forward to any participating church, even if it be liberal, depending on the Holy Spirit to take care of the one who inquired about his soul.

Thus Dr. Ferm has concluded that judging the doctrinal orthodoxy of men and churches is *forbidden, impossible* under city-wide crusade circumstances, and *unnecessary!*

He has also concluded that any minister, including a known liberal who teaches unbelief from his pulpit, by the mere virtue of his willingness to join in the campaign where the gospel is to be preached, is *"deserving"* of having converts.

The Writer's Critique

The quotation of Dr. Ferm which is given above indicates that he is under the impression that Christ has forbidden Christians from forming opinions concerning the doctrinal orthodoxy or heterodoxy of any who call themselves "Christians." His words reveal that he believes that it is against the will of Christ for Christians to judge as to whether or not a certain church or pastor will feed or starve the lambs sent to them, or whether or not the church or pastor will protect or lead astray the little ones who might be placed in their care. Since he has not stated the biblical grounds for his conclusion, it will here be conjectured that his view is most probably based upon his interpretation of Matthew 7:1, the verse which forbids judging. In any event this verse will lead us into the territory which needs exploration.

Matthew 7:1 commands, "Judge not, that ye be not judged," and the textual basis for this verse is unassailable. Arndt and Gingrich list the following meanings among the many for the verb "to judge" *(krino)* which is used twice in the verse: separate, distinguish, judge, think, consider, decide, hale before a court, condemn, administer justice, see to it that justice is done, pass judgment upon, criticize, and find fault with.[6] Despite its many shades of meaning, its parallel in Luke 6:37 which is in a context

---

6. Arndt, p. 452-53.

of being merciful versus being condemnatory, and the fuller immediate context of Matthew 7:1-4 indicate clearly that the command "Judge not" prohibits *censoriousness* with its harsh self-righteous condemnation and unmerciful spirit. The fact that the ones whom Christ deems guilty of this sin are referred to by Him as "Hypocrites" who see specks in the eyes of others while having beams in their own eyes (Matt. 7:5), shows that "faultfinding" and unmerciful despising and condemning of others is the sin at issue.

If forming opinions about others is forbidden per se, how could the Christian obey Matthew 7:6, the verse which immediately follows this subject, which commands, "Beware of false prophets," which to obey requires an opinion to be formed on the soundness of one who calls himself a prophet, or a brother. Titus 3:10 orders Christians to reject a heretic after the second admonition, and the only possible way that a Christian can obey this command is by judging the man's orthodoxy of doctrine. In 1 Corinthians 5:12 Paul's question, "Do ye not judge them that are within?" is calling for the administration of Church discipline which cannot be performed without forming an opinion about other Christians. Is Christ in John 7:24 contradicting Matthew 7:1, when in John's Gospel He utters the command which has universal application, "Judge not according to appearance, but judge righteous judgment"?

The only explanation for a resolution between the command of Matthew 7:1 and the multitude of biblical injunctions which require the forming of opinions about people, including other Christians, is to realize that Matthew 7:1 forbids censoriousness and not the necessary duty of forming opinions about persons. The alternative to this is for Christians to abandon Church discipline; to despise civil judicial proceedings against crime; to forsake any attempt to cleanse the Church; and to give up all hope of protecting the lambs from false prophets and heretics; and to assume all men to be perfectly honest.

The verse has been rightly understood to forbid censoriousness, and not to forbid the judging of others per se, by the commentators Calvin, Alford, Lenski, Barnes, Martyn Lloyd-Jones, and a myriad of other worthies. On that misinterpretation of this verse which sees any and all judging of others for any reason forbidden, Calvin declares:

> Hence it is evident, that this passage is altogether misapplied by those persons who would desire to make that moderation, which Christ recommends, a pretence for setting aside all distinction between good and evil. We are not only permitted, but are even bound, to condemn all sins; unless we choose to rebel against God himself,—nay, to repeal his laws, to reverse his decisions, and to overturn his judgment-seat. It is his will that we should proclaim the sentence that he pronounces on the actions of men: only we must preserve such modesty towards each other, as to make it manifest that he is the only Lawgiver and Judge, (Isa. xxxiii 22.)[7]

Martyn Lloyd-Jones, the able English expository preacher, in his book, *Studies in the Sermon on the Mount*, declares on the verse in question:

> Discipline, to the Protestant Fathers, was as much a mark of the Church as the preaching of the Word and the administration of the Sacraments. But we know very little about discipline. It is the result of this flabby, sentimental notion that you must not judge, and which asks, "Who are you to express judgement?" But the Scripture exhorts us to do so.
>
> This question of judging applies, also, in the matter of doctrine. Here is this question of false prophets to which our Lord calls attention. We are supposed to detect them and to avoid them. But that is impossible without a knowledge of doctrine, and the exercise of that knowledge in judgement. . . . In writing to Titus he [Paul] says, "A man that is an heretic after the first and second admonition reject." How do you know whether a man is a heretic or not if your view is that, as long as a man calls himslf a Christian, he must be a Christian, and you do not care what he believes? Then go on to John's epistles, John "the apostle of love." . . . If a man comes to you who does not hold the true doctrine, you must not receive him into your house, you must not bid him God speed and provide him with money to preach his false doctrine. But today it

---

7. Calvin, I, pp. 346-47.

would be said that that is a lack of charity, that it is being over-punctilious and censorious. This modern idea, however, is a direct contradiction of the Scripture teaching with regard to judging.[8]

Thus it is seen that the Lord did not forbid the evaluating of the doctrinal orthodoxy of men and churches, but by such admonition as, "Beware of false prophets" (Matt. 7:15), there is laid down an absolute biblical imperative for such evaluation of those who would call themselves "prophets." Thus Dr. Ferm's interpretation of the Scriptural command of the Lord in relation to judging is incorrect, and has been thought to have been incorrect by Protestant commentators from Calvin to Lloyd-Jones.

Furthermore, when Christ commanded Peter in John 21:15, "Feed my lambs," He implied the universal duty of all Christians, who in God's providence obtain positions in which they have a part in providing for younger Christians, to do everything possible for the spiritual health and welfare of Christ's lambs. This assuredly includes the concept of protection. If the evangelist who by the Holy Spirit leads the lambs into either a saving knowledge of Christ or into a desire of being saved will not be in the area to feed the lambs personally or if because of their great number he cannot possibly do the job himself, then in the face of the command of Christ he is responsible, as best he is able, to see that others who love the Lord feed the lambs. If he turns some of the lambs over to a liberal church through a mistaken view of "Christian ethics," he has betrayed the command of Christ to "Feed my lambs," and has betrayed the lambs who trust his guidance and protection. He has failed the Lord and the lambs by not obeying the command, "Beware of false prophets" (Matt. 7:15)—for the lambs are yet not mature enough to recognize for themselves the danger and the wickedness of the unbelief of modernism. To sidestep his duty as an undershepherd of the sheep by saying piously, "The same Holy Spirit must be trusted to perfect that which he has begun,"[9] does not excuse his disobedience to a clearly commanded obligation.

When Satan told Christ to cast Himself off the pinnacle of the Temple, Christ said, "It is written again, Thou shalt not tempt the

---

8. D. Martyn Lloyd-Jones, *Studies in the Sermon on the Mount* (2 vols.; Grand Rapids: Eerdmans Publishing Co., 1960), II, 164-65.

9. Ferm, p. 19.

Lord thy God" (Matt. 4:7). Dr. Ferm's excuse, which is not the excuse of Dr. Ferm only, is attempting to justify the disobedient evangelist's placing the young lambs for whom Christ shed His blood *in a known and scripturally warned against danger* on the grounds that the Holy Spirit has promised in Philippians 1:6 to protect them. This is tempting God unnecessarily, and is precisely what Satan suggested to Christ when he said, "Cast thyself down" (Matt. 4:5). In this case the Holy Spirit will have to perform his promise to those truly saved by using one cause or another to bring them out of the liberal church and into sound churches where they can grow in Christ without the poisoning influence of liberalism and rationalism. Those who have made inquiries but who are not as yet saved, by being channeled into a liberal church, humanly speaking, will be deprived of the opportunity of going on into belief as long as they remain there because of the human rationalistic unbelief which they will be cleverly fed.

Thus Dr. Ferm's ideas advocate disobedience by the evangelist to his biblical obligation of protecting the lambs on the grounds that the Holy Spirit will protect them. He advocates that the commands written by the Spirit, the ultimate author of the Word of God, be disobeyed on the grounds of the Spirit's written promise of protection! However, such disobedience to the commands of the Spirit, deprive the Spirit of one of the God-ordained means by which He, the Spirit, performs His promise!

It cannot be sidestepped, the biblical imperative exists which makes necessary the judgment of the doctrinal orthodoxy or heterodoxy of those to whom an evangelist contemplates entrusting the lambs of God. The evangelist does not discharge his duty by allowing liberals who cooperate with him to take any of these little ones into their folds. He can only discharge this obligation (John 21:15) by refusing to allow modernists to cooperate in the work of the Lord and thus by example not approving of them, and by warning the lambs of the unbelieving ones who would as grievous wolves kill their souls with unbelief if allowed (Acts 20:26-31).

On Dr. Ferm's speaking of a ". . . cooperative effort, where the Gospel is to be preached without restrictions of any kind, . . ." it must again be asserted that in a "cooperative effort" which finds a conservative preacher sponsored by many who are liberal, there is a tremendous restriction![10] That restriction is the understood agreement that the one who is sponsored will not attack his sponsors, which in this case effectively means that he will not denounce the unbelief of modernism as sin, he will not cry "Woe" unto the "blind leaders," and he will not warn the sheep and the lambs of Christ to beware of the insidious dangers of false prophets as did the Lord (Matt. 7:15) and the Apostle Paul (Acts 20:26-30).

As to the alleged impossibility of the evangelist's deciding upon the doctrinal soundness of churches and workers who wish to participate in the campaign, it may be said that a simple required signing of a creedal statement which asserts the truth, reality, and historicity of the fundamentals of the faith would take care of this entire matter, would satisfy the critics of Dr. Graham, and would discharge the evangelist's sacred obligation to the Lord.

Is it difficult to decide whether a particular church or religious body is sound or heretical? Dr. Graham and Dr. Robert O. Ferm declare that the difficulty is overwhelming. Dr. Graham has said, "No group of ministers in any large city anywhere in the world agree on what constitutes a sound church."[11] Dr. Ferm declares, ". . . it would be impossible to set up a local committee that would agree on which churches are worthy [to participate in a cooperative evangelistic crusade] and which are not."[12] To Dr. Graham's remark, Dr. Bob Jones, Sr., replied:

> I have been in evangelistic work for sixty years, having started when I was just a boy; and wherever I have held a meeting, any pastor in the town or city could tell me any time I would ask about a church, "It is (or is not) a sound church with an orthodox pastor." All Americans do not agree about some things . . . but . . . Every orthodox Christian in the world believes that the Bible is the Word of God and whatever it says is so, and they all agree that it says that the Lord Jesus Christ was born of a virgin; He was God manifest in the flesh; He died a vicarious, substitutionary death on the cross; He bodily arose from the dead; and He is the world's only Saviour.[13]

---

10. *Ibid.*

11. "Dr. Bob Jones Writes about Graham's New York Crusade," *A Ministry of Disobedience* (Collingswood: Christian Beacon Press, 1957), p. 47.

12. Ferm, p. 19.

13. *A Ministry of Disobedience* (Collingswood: Christian Beacon Press, 1957), p. 47.

It is to be noted that Dr. Graham speaks of a *sound* church, Dr. Ferm talks of a *worthy* church, and Dr. Jones speaks of a *sound* church using the fundamentals of the Historic Christian Faith as his criterion of soundness. If Dr. Graham uses the word "sound" as a synonym for Dr. Ferm's "worthy," and if "worthy" means "deserving" then truly only the Lord could decide with absolute certainty, for mortal men in this life cannot with ultimate finality pronounce on who is *deserving* and who is not *deserving* of the blessing of being allowed to participate in an evangelistic crusade or other work of the Lord. However, such participation is not to be considered as a desert for the *worthy* or *deserving*, but as a *duty* to be performed by the Church. Thus it is seen that because mortal Christians must judge by outward fruits and are not able to peer into the hearts of men or organizations, except in clear cases of unmistakable piety or profligacy, the evaluation of anyone's or any group's *worthiness* is a subjective matter, which may well occasion disagreement.

However, the matter of *soundness* is not so subjective. If *soundness* be taken in the usual sense, as Dr. Jones, Sr., used it, then it refers to orthodoxy of doctrine. This can be objectively evaluated by comparing the creedal statements of a group and its oral and written teachings with the fundamental docrtines of the Historic Christian Faith. This task is not so difficult as it might appear because just as the Church must acknowledge one who gives a credible profession as a member of the visible Church, being unable to look into the heart, so must any group be considered sound that has an orthodox creedal profession and teaching. Heart searching and the issue of *worthiness* are here excluded and only the outward manifestations are evaluated. Thus the groups which are to be considered as sound are the ones who *profess* to believe in the fundamental doctrines and whose teaching maintains that these doctrines are true, despite the beliefs or doubts to which they *may secretly* cling. The societies which are to be evaluated as heretical are those who openly *voice* adherence to such doctrines as are heterodox, or who *voice* their doubt of the truth of one of the fundamental doctrines of the faith.

Since, the evaluation of who is sound and who is heretical, depends not on heart searching but on "listening to voices," this process must be acknowledged as objective and attainable! Thus a group of fundamental Christians may come together and study the teachings of a person or a group and declare that the person or group professes to believe and teaches the fundamental tenets of the Christian religion, and is therefore to be considered sound doctrinally. Likewise they may, after study, declare that a person or society teaches heterodox views and unbelief, and is therefore to be considered heretical doctrinally. In a large crusade the requiring of the signing of a creedal statement affirming belief in the great fundamentals of the faith by churches and workers who wish to participate would take care of the situation.

Conclusions

It has been seen in this section that the Lord's commandment, "Judge not, that ye be not judged" (Matt. 7:1), was directed against self-righteous unmerciful censoriousness, and that in no sense does it forbid the forming of opinions about men and movements which is absolutely vital in order to obey the many commands in Scripture which call upon the believer to discriminate between good and evil and to act differently with respect to them. In this case, it has been observed that there is a solemn and sacred duty of judging who are false prophets and of bewaring of them in one's own life and of protecting God's lambs from them. This has been the uniform Protestant opinion among the orthodox commentators from Calvin to the present.

The impossibility and the unnecessariness of evaluating the orthodoxy of men which is affirmed by the New Evangelicals has been shown to be the exact opposite of the biblical admonitions which place upon an evangelist the obligation to care for and to feed God's lambs. It has been seen that the neglect of this duty is a sinful crime of omission in light of the scripturally founded duties of every undershepherd. Also, it has been noted that the only way for the evangelist to adequately protect the lambs is by his not entering upon a cooperative relationship with liberals which binds him to keep silent on the sin of modernism and which prevents him from discharging his sacred duty of warning the lambs against the wolves.

47

Thus the sixth argument which maintains that judging the doctrinal soundness of men and churches is forbidden by the Lord, and in this case unnecessary and impossible, is seen to fall on every one of its allegations.

ARGUMENT VII

"The Lord Did Not Make an Issue out of Theological Error"

The Argument Advanced by Dr. Ferm

The seventh anti-separatist proposition states that the Lord's stress negatively was against hypocrisy and bigotry and not against theological error, and therefore, the evangelist's negative stress ought also to be against hypocrisy and bigotry, and not against doctrinal unbelief. In line with this Dr. Ferm asserts the following:

> The numerous occasions when the ministry of our Lord brought him in contact with persons of unorthodox belief or improper morals all reveal his supreme passion. . . . On no occasion did he inquire concerning the theology or even the conduct of those to whom he went to minister. . . . one who reads the record of the New Testament will discover that Jesus attacked hypocrisy and bigotry more than any other evil.[1]

An Examination of Dr. Ferm's Conclusions

As the conclusions of the author of *Cooperative Evangelism* are evaluated they must be considered in the light of his purpose of justifying an inclusive policy of conducting evangelistic crusades and Christian work in general. In this case Dr. Ferm has concluded that Christ concerned Himself negatively with hypocrisy and not orthodoxy of doctrine, and therefore orthodoxy of doctrine should not be a matter of great concern for the conservative evangelist of today. However, with his words, "On no occasion did he [the Lord] inquire concerning the theology or even the conduct of those to whom he went to minister," Dr. Ferm seems to have applied his alleged findings concerning Christ's indifference to the orthodoxy of those *"to whom"* he went to minister, to those *"with whom"* the conservative cooperative evangelist ministers.[2] If this is denied then he would be arguing for an evangelist's not having to inquire as to the orthodoxy of those in the pews to

---

1. *Ibid.,* p. 35.
2. *Ibid.*

whom the gospel message is being addressed; and he could not be arguing for this, for no one, be he a separatist or not, has ever maintained that one who does not yet believe must adhere to the fundamentals in order to be allowed to sit in the pews and be preached to as an unconverted sinner. Thus Dr. Ferm seems to have concluded on the basis of Christ's alleged conduct toward the unconverted, that the evangelist need not ascertain the orthodoxy or heterodoxy of the ones "*with whom*" he cooperates, and therefore, cooperating with modernists is legal.

It is evident that Dr. Ferm has also concluded that the Christian preacher of today must not stress negatively any sin more than the Lord stressed that same sin, regardless of how the contemporary situation might differ from that of the Lord's day. This is the reasoning which undergirds his concept that since our Lord did not stress the evil of heterodoxy (which point has assuredly not been established by proof), the evangelist of today would be wrong to stress it.

The Writer's Critique

"On no occasion did he [the Lord] inquire concerning the theology or even the conduct of those to whom he went to minister," is a remarkable statement for Dr. Ferm or anyone to utter.

In John 4 Jesus is found ministering to the Samaritan woman, and He here both inquires into her conduct and points out error in her theology. His words to her, "Go, call thy husband, and come hither" (John 4:16), are the beginning of Christ's inquiry into her immoral conduct of life, and they result in the Lord's exposing her past sin and her present living with one who is not her husband, thus establishing within her conscience her sinfulness and need of forgiveness (John 4:16-18). After she displays her theological ignorance Christ exposes her error clearly by saying, "Ye worship ye know not what: we know what we worship: for salvation is of the Jews" (John 4:22). This mirrors the fact that the Lord's purpose in teaching mankind was to set their conduct aright in the sight of God and to set their theology aright in the light of His person and work and the entire compass of God's dealings with man. Dr. Ferm's statement causes us to miss the point that

50

Christ was *vitally concerned* with conduct and theology, and when He did not inquire of the people "*to whom*" He went to minister, it was primarily because all of the lost are presumed to be incorrect in both conduct and theology as in fact they are, and they are in need of complete instruction in both of these vital areas. The children of God "*to whom*" He went to minister were not inquired of because they in their true belief and practice of Judaism and its one true God displayed their orthodoxy of belief and their uprightness of life with regards to the Old Testament. To these He taught the new light and they saw it and were glad!

However, is it true that he did not inquire into the conduct or theology of those "*with whom*" he came to minister? His disciples really were His students and assistants at once. The entire ministry of the Savior toward them was to set their conduct and theology aright so that they could teach others primarily after His resurrection! Except for Judas Iscariot, who will be discussed shortly, did not Christ pick orthodox, though not faultless, Jewish men to be His disciples? Witness Peter's declaration when in Acts 10 the Lord commands him to "Kill and eat," of the unclean animals upon the heavenly sheet (Acts 10:10-13). Peter says, "Not so, Lord: for I have *never* eaten any thing that is common or unclean" (Acts 10:14). Except for Judas Iscariot, there is no hint in the New Testament that any of the twelve were "liberal Jews" who doubted the Mosaic authorship of the Pentateuch, who thought that the J Document was a vestige of an ancient folklore or who believed that Trito-Isaiah completed the Book of Isaiah.

With regard to Judas, the study of which alone could occupy more than one doctoral dissertation, after Christ announced His betrayal by one of the twelve, they each "began every one of them to say unto him, Lord is it I?" (Matt. 26:22). This shows that the other eleven did not necessarily suspect that the one trusted with the moneybag was a traitor, thus informing the readers of the New Testament that Judas' outward profession was orthodox, and that only the Lord knew that he was a tare among the wheat. The solution of the quandary seems to lie in the fact that the Lord in His humanity, that is, acting like a mortal man, chose Judas as a disciple on the basis of his acceptable outward profession, all the while knowing in His divine nature that this was to be the traitor. Christ, here acted like a common man who judges by the external appearance, so that among the many purposes in the mind of God for this selection, Christ could be the example to every Christian undershepherd who is betrayed by one of his fellow laborers who was chosen by virtue of his sound and orthodox external profession. So even in the case of Iscariot, Christ did not bring along a co-worker who was a liberal heretic by profession, for Judas was an orthodox faithful follower of Christ to all mortal eyes. Once, however, Judas showed outwardly his true color he was immediately rejected!

Since Christ never came before the public as a co-worker, a cooperator with, or as a preacher sponsored by the unbelieving Pharisees and the heterodox Sadducees, no argument based on them is valid that declares that an evangelist today does not need to inquire of his co-workers concerning these matters. This is true because Christ continually, as it has been established earlier in this monograph, rebuked the Pharisees for their formalistic dead legalism and for their heterodoxical unbelief in Christ's messiahship and the strife between Christ and them issued in blood, the death of the Lord. It is true because concerning the doctrine of the Sadducees, Christ openly proclaimed their error with His words, "Ye do err, not knowing the scriptures, nor the power of God" (Matt. 22:29; 22:23-33), and warned men to beware of their leaven (Matt. 16:6).

Thus Dr. Ferm's statement, "On no occasion did he [the Lord] inquire concerning the theology or even the conduct of those *to whom* [italics mine] he went to minister," is seen to be of questionable accuracy, to suggest improper grounds for the false inference that the Lord was not concerned with these areas, and to not apply at all to the Lord's policy with respect to those *with whom* He came to minister nor to the Lord's desires with respect to those *with whom* an orthodox Christian worker cooperates.

The second statement which requires examination in this section is Dr. Ferm's assertion, "Nevertheless [i.e., in spite of the sectarian divisions of the Hebrew religion] one who reads the record of the New Testament will discover that Jesus attacked hypocrisy and bigotry more than any other evil."[3] Dr. Ferm's reasoning here, in line with the context of his writing which is to defend cooperative evangelism, seeks to assert that (1) Jesus attacked hypocrisy more than any other sin, (2) therefore, evangelists when not preaching the gospel per se should make the thrust of their "negative" condemnation of sin against hypocrisy and not against modernism and unbelief, and (3) therefore any evangelist or Christian worker who is not speaking out against unbelief in the liberal churches, but who is denouncing hypocrisy in general, is not only blameless, but is in fact following the precise example of the Lord. This would seem to fairly represent the thrust of the argument of Dr. Ferm's words.

The basic error in the reasoning above lies in its misapplication of an implied general rule which states that, "The preacher of today in his preaching, all things being equal, is wise to devote approximately the same proportion of time to each biblical subject as the New Testament devotes to that subject." Dr. Ferm's reasoning calls for an ironclad adherence to this general maxim, and justifies the cooperative evangelist's not speaking out against modernism on the grounds that the Scriptures, in this case only the pre-resurrection ministry of the Lord, do not devote a substantial proportion of time to this particular theme; and on the contrary, he implies, that fundamentalists ought to spend more time speaking against hypocrisy instead of unbelief.

There are, however, several points of issue which can be taken with this line of thought—which, incidentally, is not a "straw man" but the very reasoning behind the thrust of the statement which is being analyzed in this section.

The first item involves the fact that the general rule of preaching emphasis is predicated upon the circumstance of "All things being equal," which words are included in the above statement of the rule. This takes into consideration the fact that there is another rule concerning preaching emphasis which goes along with the one just mentioned. This additional rule states that, "A minister is bound before the Lord to emphasize any subject which the congregation to whom he speaks needs to have emphasized to

---

3. *Ibid.*

them because of the circumstances of their present situation." The guidance for this emphasis should come from the Holy Spirit working in the preacher's heart as he prayerfully considers his congregation's current situation in light of the Scriptures which have been authored by the Spirit. His, the speaker's manifold obligations to glorify God by vindicating His truth against falsehood, error, and unbelief, to warn the wicked to repent (Ezek. 33:8), to preach the Good Tidings to the lost, to instruct the Church in all things, to strengthen and feed the flock of God (John 21:15-17), to warn the flock of God against wolves (Acts 20: 26-31), and to protect the little ones (John 21:15; 10:12), can only be discharged by the preacher's making clear the mind of God, which is found in the Scriptures, on any given subject when the *need* arises.

Thus Dr. Ferm's thrust does not take into consideration the *need* of the hour which exists because today's world is rapidly falling away into unbelief and because the liberal Protestant churches are one of the great agents of Satan for advancing the ideas that a Godless evolution is responsible for our existence, that the Old Testament is a patchwork of pseudonymed documents expressing a morality of a tyrannical antiquity, that Christ was not born of a virgin, did not do miraculous acts, did not actually bodily arise from the grave, that hell is a figment of the early Church's imagination rather than the eternal abode of the lost, and that the social gospel needs the Christians' commitment in view of the fact that the fundamentalist dichotomy of the saved and the lost is a fanciful relic of an uninspired Bible.

Dr. Ferm's thrust does not take into consideration the great *need* that the new inquirers and converts have of being warned to stay away from the influence of the great liberal churches, nor does it take away from the influence of the liberal churches, nor does it take into account the great sin of omission which an evangelist commits when he approves of the worthiness of liberal clerics by asking them to pray in public, as if God would bless *because* of the prayers of a heretic, and by so doing, not only fails to warn the lambs of the wolf, but encourages the lambs to trust the wolf for their sustenance. Thus, the *need* of the moment at evangelistic meetings is not only the preaching of the saving Gospel, but also the warning of the sheep. The *need* of preaching against hypocrisy to babes in Christ with tears of decision in their eyes does not exist in comparison to the desperate *need* for these little ones to be warned against Satan's most effective means of stunting their spiritual growth which is through the leaven of unbelief sown in the liberal churches. The *need* of speaking against hypocrisy to inquirers, who though not yet saved desire to learn more of the Savior's work, does not exist in comparison to the *need* of warning these of the liberal churches who while coveting their "membership" are haunted by Satan's fowls who desire to steal away the tiny seed of faith within the inquirer's breast (Matt. 13:4,19).

Dr. Ferm's thrust neglects the weighty obligation that a conservative evangelist has to vindicate the truth of God by giving the lie to the unbelief of the liberals and by denouncing them as false prophets. Can a conservative who cooperates with and approves of false prophets instead of denouncing their sin, excuse himself to God by claiming that he preaches against other sins? Is it not hypocrisy to appear as a prophet of the one true God and at the same time fellowship with the false prophets who question the very historicity of the conservative's God? The *need* here is not for the preaching against hypocrisy in general, but for the preaching against the hypocrisy of the wicked unbelief of the pious-looking modernists who destroy the souls of men with their lies.

Thus Dr. Ferm's preaching emphasis thrust must be critiqued on the grounds that it has forgotten the obligation a conservative evangelist has to the Savior that redeemed his soul to emphasize whatever matter is *needed* in order to faithfully vindicate God's truth against the unbelieving clerics and in order to meet the need that the lambs have of being warned against the modernist wolves. In this case preaching the Gospel is not the only need, and the doing of this good thing does not clear an evangelist from unfaithfulness in meeting the needs of the hour! In short, Dr. Ferm's point has neglected the necessity of preaching to meet *all* of the important *needs* of the hearers!

Another item to be noted is that the using of the Lord's ministry as a basis for emphasis in today's preaching must be done so with discernment. The Pharisees who were the legalists of the day were Christ's primary enemies, making themselves such, and one of their great sins was hypocrisy. Their hypocrisy was centered about a false estimate of their own self-righteousness based upon a legalistic rather than a redemptory concept of obtaining righteousness. This caused them to despise others, and to hate Christ for pointing out their own sinful condition. This in turn caused them *to reject Christ* as the Messiah, and to *disbelieve* in Him. *Thus their hypocrisy which was built upon a false nonredemptive theology, was in turn linked together with unbelief.*

The modernists of today are extremely similar to the Pharisees in certain respects![4] They account themselves to be righteous on the basis of their ethical standards and attainments believing themselves to be following the "ethical" and the "social" Christ, and at the same time, by their rejecting the historicity of the resurrection and of the substitutionary atonement they show themselves to trust in their own righteousness, and not in the righteousness of the Cross. Thus they too are the Pharisees, self-righteous false shepherds. By posing as lovers of God and His Christ while trusting in their own righteousness they prove to be false prophets in that they teach others an erroneous and false view of God; and also to be hypocrites, in that they pretend to have achieved righteousness before God when in truth they are full of unrighteousness. They are pious frauds! *Thus it is seen that while the Pharisees' unbelief in Christ stemmed from a hypocrisy which was rooted in a non-redemptive false theology of works, the hypocrisy of the liberals stems from their unbelief; and both are similar in that they are each guilty of both self-righteous hypocrisy and unbelief in Jesus as the Christ!*

Out of the twenty New Testament occurrences of the words "hypocrisy," *hupokrisis* and "hypocrite(s)," *hupokritas*, thirteen

---

4. Those who say that the fundamentalists of today are similar to the Pharisees because they both judge, err by not seeing the vast chasm between the sinful judging of the Pharisees on the basis of their own self-righteousness and the righteous judging by fundamentalists against liberals and Jehosaphats who aid the liberals (2 Chron. 19:2) on the basis of biblical commands to reject heretics (Titus 3:10) and to have no fellowship with the unbelieving deniers of God (2 Cor. 6:14-1:1).

clearly refer to either the Pharisees alone or with others, and in the seven other unspecified occurrences the Pharisees are most likely included.[5] Thus the condemnation of Christ against the Pharisees who were hypocrites cannot be so quickly isolated from their unbelief for the two always traveled together. In like manner, if Dr. Ferm desires modern day hypocrisy condemned, it must be condemned foremost in the camp of the worst offenders, and these are the liberals of today! However, their hypocrisy is a result of their unbelief, and whosoever condemns the one must denounce the other! The liberal is a "hypocrite" on the basis of his external piety in the face of his *unbelief* in the substitutionary atonement! Dr. Ferm's desire to see hypocrisy condemned as the Lord condemned it, must take into account that the Lord's condemnation of the hypocrites of His day, the Pharisees, cannot be isolated from the Lord's condemnation of the unbelievers of His day—for the Pharisees were guilty synonymously of both hypocrisy and unbelief.

A final item to be noted with regard to Dr. Ferm's thrust concerning emphasis is that the real issue at the heart of the matter is not "What did the Lord spend the most time on?" as Dr. Ferm centers the issue on. The question is did the Lord and the New Testament condemn the sin of unbelief in those who call themselves Christ's prophets, and do Christ and the New Testament actually charge Christians to beware of false prophets, to put heretics out of the Church, and to save the little lambs from the fangs of unbelieving teachers? If the Lord and the New Testament did so, and they did (Matt. 7:15; Titus 3:10; John 21:15; Acts 20:26-31; Rom. 16:17; 2 Cor. 6:14-7:1; 2 John 10,11; Jude 3,4; etc.), then the liberal heretics must be condemned and warned against as often as necessary in addition to the proclaiming of the Gospel and other teachings of the Bible.

If a tribal pastor's congregation in Africa is in danger of reverting to cannibalism, the question is not, "How much time did the Lord specifically devote in His preaching to warning of the evils of cannibalism?" but "Is cannibalism condemned in the New

---

5. Robert Young, *Analytical Concordance to the Bible* (21st American ed. revised; New York: Funk & Wagnalls Co., n.d.), p. 506.

Testament either by direct precept or by clear inference?" If the answer to the latter question is affirmative, which it obviously is, the preacher may preach on the topic as much as is necessary. The Holy Spirit who condemned that sin in the Scriptures will lead the preacher in his words if the preacher but yields himself, and no man dare rise and ask, "How much time did Jesus spend on this specific topic?" for anything and everything that is condemned as sin in the Bible, is condemned as such by the Holy Spirit, and the Lord Jesus being of the same Godhead as the Holy Spirit also does agree with the condemnation.

Thus it is seen that whatever sin the Bible condemns, in this case unbelief in the clergy, Christ and the Spirit also condemn whether or not the Lord specifically stressed it in His contemporary circumstances. However, let no one say that the Lord who said, "Beware of false prophets" (Matt. 7:15), would be pleased to see an argument based upon His ministry used to rebuke those Christians who cry, "Beware of false prophets!"

Conclusions

Thus it has been seen in this section that the fact that Christ during His ministry denounced the Pharisaical hypocrites continually, cannot biblically, properly, or logically be used as the basis for an argument which excuses any evangelist for not speaking against the unbelief of liberalism and for not warning the little ones who come forward because of his preaching of the Gospel against the modernistic wolves who would harm their souls. This has been observed to be true primarily because it has been seen that the Christ who denounced the hypocrites during His earthly ministry, also joins the Holy Spirit, the ultimate author of all of Scriptures, in the unity of the Trinity, in condemning unbelieving religious teachers who are false prophets. This condemnation of unbelief, which has been shown to be the need of the hour, has been seen to be not contrary to the condemnation of hypocrisy in Christ's earthly sojourn, but in accord with it. Thus the seventh New Evangelical argument advocates a false emphasis at the expense of that which is truly needed in this hour, and therefore, it must be rejected.

ARGUMENT VIII

"The Lord Stressed Fellowship, Not Separation"

The Argument Advanced by Dr. Ferm

The eighth New Evangelical contention is made as follows:

> Mr. Frank Colquhoun, of the Evangelical Alliance in London, after a careful study of separation and fellowship in the New Testament, has concluded that "the Bible lays more emphasis upon fellowship than upon mere negative separation." This being the case, it is safer, as a rule, to seek to cooperate unless cooperation affords no open door. Therefore the missionary or evangelist takes no risk in practicing a cooperative policy.[1]

An Examination of Dr. Ferm's Conclusions

In a way very similar to that discussed in Argument Seven, where preaching against hypocrisy in general was made the antithesis of preaching against doctrinal error when actually both have their proper place, here practicing fellowship and practicing separation have been made antithetical actions. On the basis of this choice between the two, Dr. Ferm states that he agrees that fellowship is the practice stressed in the New Testament, and that therefor this is "safer, as a rule." He further concludes on the basis of fellowship being stressed more than separation, that, "The missionary or evangelist takes no risk in practicing a cooperative policy."[2]

Dr. Ferm's conclusion here, which is exhibited in his coinage of an "It is safer . . . to seek to cooperate"[3] rule of thumb, displays the fact that the conclusions on the matter of ecclesiastical separation which he advocates are not delineated by a careful stipulation of the biblical conditions of fellowship and of separation, but are based on a blanket conviction that "What the Bible

---

1. Ferm, p. 35, quoting Frank Colquhoun, *The Fellowship of the Gospel* (Grand Rapids: Zondervan Publishing House, 1957), p. 34.

2. *Ibid.*

3. *Ibid.*

emphasizes ought to be followed." This truism like any truism can be eloquently and loudly defended, but unless it is acted upon with the stabilizing reservation that it is to be followed only under the circumstances under which God intended it to be followed, its good emphasis when misapplied only results in much evil and confusion.

The Writer's Critique

Again, as before, it is necessary to orientate this proposition with the aim of Dr. Ferm's book, which is to present a defense and rationale for the neo-evangelical position of inclusivism which in evangelism places together conservatives and liberals on the same platform. In this proposition this policy is defended on the grounds that the New Testament stresses fellowship more than it stresses separation, and therefore "it is safer, as a rule, to seek to cooperate unless cooperation affords no open door."[4]

It first must be observed that the New Testament commands quite strongly that true Christians ought to especially love one another just as Christ has loved them (John 13:34,35). However, it also must be noted that the New Testament also speaks of the duty of a Christian to *avoid* those "which cause divisions and offenses contrary to the doctrine" (Rom. 16:17), to *reject* heretics (Titus 3:10), to *beware of* false prophets (Matt. 3:10), to *receive not* one who proclaims a doctrine which is not the doctrine of Christ (2 John 10,11), to "*let him be accursed*" who brings another gospel (Gal. 1:8,9), to *not be unequally yoked with* unbelievers, *to touch them not,* and to *come out from among them* (2 Cor. 6:14-7:1). In addition to this, there is the example of the Lord in Matt. 23 calling the Pharisees "Children of hell" (v. 15), "Hypocrites" (vv. 13,15,23,25,27, and 29), "Fools and blind" (v. 19), "Full of extortion and excess" (v. 25), "Full of dead bones, and of uncleanliness (v. 27), "Full of hypocrisy and iniquity (v. 28), "Serpents," "Generation of vipers" (v. 33), ones heading for the damnation of hell (v. 33), "Blind guides" (v. 24), and "Children of them which killed the prophets" (v. 31).

---

4. Ferm, p. 35.

Thus it appears that while Christians are to love one another so sincerely that all men shall know by beholding their mutual love that they are the disciples of Christ (John 13:34,35), and while they are also to love even their enemies who curse them (Matt. 6:44), they are on the other hand commanded to manifest a conduct of separation toward those who are in the group of false prophets, heretics, causers of divisions contrary to the received doctrine, unbelievers, and advocates of another gospel or of another Christ. This separation is to manifest itself toward these by such actions as avoidance, rejection, severing yokes, severing relationships, non-fellowship, non-reception into the house, a wary and cautious posture toward them and a sincere inner hope that the purposes of such false believers and teachers as well as the parties themselves will meet with their just end (Rom. 16:17; Titus 3:10; 2 Cor. 6:14 - 7:1; 2 John 10,11; Matt: 7:15; and Gal. 1:8,9).

Although Christians ought to love each other for many reasons, they are to especially love each other because they know that God, who is the supreme object of their love, Himself loves their fellow disciples (1 John 4:11). This love they are to manifest outwardly in every possible way. Likewise, because the Holy God hateth "all workers of iniquity." [Lit. "You have hated . . ."] (Psa. 5:5), Christians must also be set against sin, its advocates, and prophets—notwithstanding their constant hope and prayer that these might repent and change their allegiance. Christians for this reason are in a true sense the enemies of all ungodly purposes and teachings and are bound never to aid anyone in a work for Satan. Thus Jehu rebuked Jehosaphat, who was basically a man of God, for aiding ungodly Ahab by an alliance (2 Chron. 19:2,3). So it can be seen that the people of God are to express universal love, especially for each other, but as they truly love God's holiness, goodness, and righteousness, their love for these must also manifest itself in abhorrence and hatred for sin, sinful deeds and purposes, and the advocating of evil schemes!

Applying these truths to the subject at hand, it is seen that the New Testament calls for the manifesting by Christians of the utmost in fellowship and cooperation toward those who profess Christ and who are not holding or bringing pernicious doctrine and error, nor living in immorality or other open sin; while it on the other hand calls for a distinct separation from fellowship, approval, cooperation and the giving of aid towards those who are heretical, because, ". . . he that biddeth him [the heretic who abideth not in the doctrine of Christ] God speed is partaker of his evil deeds" (2 John 11). The Lord's ministry exhibited this duality of conduct for which the Scriptures call! To the disciples and the children of God, the Lord showed approval and love, but to those who were the false teachers who in unbelief rejected Him, Christ manifested open rebuke and scorn (Matt. 23). *The commands with regard to each of the two groups are absolutely unflagging in their posture and emphasis, so that anyone who treats one group as he ought to have treated the other makes a grave and serious mistake, and if anyone does this intentionally it is wicked direct disobedience to God's Word in the most profligate way.* Therefore, it behooves each Christian when he comes into contact with a heretic to beware of, avoid, and reject him,[5] and not to cooperate with, approve of, and aid him!

Now to compare this with Dr. Ferm's words. He writes:

> This being the case [i.e., the assertion that the Bible stresses fellowship more than separation], it is safer, as a rule, to seek to cooperate unless cooperation affords no open door. Therefore the missionary or evangelist takes no risk in practicing a cooperative policy.[6]

In the face of the New Testament's emphatic demands for an extremely different conduct from the Christian toward the brethren and toward the heretics, Dr. Ferm sidesteps the issue which centers around the friendly and cooperative treatment given to liberal

---

5. The heretic, of course, is not to be rejected until he has had his two admonitions (Titus 3:10,11). However, two admonitions from each and every Christian is not the sense of the text, but what is required is two grave official admonitions from the Church's representatives.

6. Ferm, p. 35.

heretics by the champions of cooperative evangelism, and says that "It is safer, as a rule, to seek to cooperate"! This would be a good rule if there were no identifying marks to the heretic, and if Christians were to look squarely in the eye of each religious leader who wished to participate in a campaign and on the basis of this deep gaze were to *guess* whether this was a true brother or a heretic. However, this is not the case! Christians cannot search hearts and are not commanded to do so; and therefore, all who profess to be true and who do not deny this by word or deed are to be presumed as true Christians and brethren.

However, those who by their preaching or writing, publicly display unbelief in the fundamentals of the faith such as the bodily resurrection, the virgin birth, the substitutionary atonement, etc., which is the unbelief called "modernism," have shown themselves to be heretical and are to be treated accordingly. There is no more doubt in their case. There is no guessing or looking into hearts, which is not the prerogative of the Christian, but the clear revelation that these are false teachers, unbelievers, false prophets, and therefore ones which must not be allowed to obtain possession of God's flock, especially His lambs. These are to be separated from as the Bible unflaggingly commands, and Christians are to display the same rebuking attitude toward them that the Lord displayed to the Christ-rejecting Pharisees in Matthew 23. They by their unbelief, and their teaching and advocacy of the same, have revealed themselves to be enemies of Christ and His Church and all of their claims of love to Christ are shown to be false by their wicked profession of unbelief. In this they are seen to be wolves in sheep's clothing, self-righteous hypocritical pious frauds who will only lead God's flock astray if allowed.

The cooperative evangelist is disobedient to the Scripture when he does not display this attitude of rebuke and warning to the liberals, and by his cooperating with them and approving of them before the public, his disobedience is openly rebellious to God's revealed will. Dr. Ferm's words, "Therefore the missionary or evangelist takes no risk in practicing a cooperative policy," set aside the Bible's commands for a discrimination between brethren and heretics and places its stamp of approval on a policy of insubordination to the Word of God on this issue.[7]

Dr. Ferm's words, ". . . it is safer, as a rule, to seek to cooperate *unless cooperation affords no open door* [italics mine]," reflects an improper criterion for cooperation. The Bible's criterion calls for cooperation with a brother who is of sound doctrine and of an orderly life. Complete harmony on denominational distinctives and minor matters is not required. It is not a criterion based upon opportunity; not even opportunity to do good or to preach the Gospel. The ends do not justify the means, for the Lord would have gained a greater opportunity to preach in Jewry if He had confined His healings to the six non-sabbatical days, but He on countless occasions sacrificed opportunity in order to heal a person on the Sabbath when He could easily have healed them on the day before or after. He did this because *doing right* was His criterion of action, and in this case the right thing was to deliver a bound person on God's Day and cause the hypocrisy of the Pharisees to be exposed and rebuked.

One final point must be again noted. Dr. Ferm's words, ". . . as long as he [the cooperative evangelist] declares to them [his hearers] the whole counsel of God," reveals his apparent conclusion that an evangelist who has liberals on his sponsoring committee can and actually does, in the case of Dr. Graham, preach the whole counsel of God.[8] Since in the meetings conducted by the cooperative evangelist liberals are not rebuked nor are the people warned against them, it would seem that Dr. Ferm does not see this as being included under the heading, "The whole counsel of God." Or, perhaps, the apologists of the inclusive policy in their zeal to tell the fundamentalists that even though they are cooperating with liberals they are yet preaching only the conservative's Christ, actually simply forgot that there is included in the whole counsel of God the warning against grievous wolves (Acts 20:26-31)!

7. *Ibid.*

8. *Ibid.*

Conclusions

It has been seen that the Bible clearly and emphatically calls for (1) love and its resultant union and cooperation under one set of circumstances, that is between true and sound believers, and for (2) rebuke, warning against, and separation under another set of circumstances, that is, between believers and heretics. Also it has been observed that since Christians have neither the duty nor the ability to search out the secrets of the heart, professing Christians must be presumed to be orthodox unless and until they expose themselves as heretics by their words and teachings. With these facts in mind, it has been noted that those who openly avow the unbelief of modernism are to be treated not with the approval, cooperation, and fellowship with which cooperative evangelism accords them, but with public rebuke and separation. Inasmuch as Dr. Ferm's proposition advocates a general rule of cooperation, without regard to the Scriptural distinction between true and false brethren, it is seen that his rule does not truly represent the biblical teaching on the subject. It has been further noted that his advocacy of a general probability rule, which neglects the required looking into the circumstances under which cooperation is to be rendered, sidesteps the real issue between fundamentalism and cooperative evangelism. That issue is centered upon the fact that the cooperative evangelist displays public approval of *known* (*not*: "possible " or "suspected") modernists, who are heretics, and places them in positions of fellowship and trust which actions are disobedient to the revealed will of God as it is inscripturated.

Thus the assertions which comprise the eighth proposition of Dr. Ferm avoid the issue at hand and advance a generality which when completely followed as advocated leads to disobedience on the part of Christians which displeases God. Therefore the eighth proposition must be rejected.

ARGUMENT IX

"The Lord's Method Was to Proclaim the Truth and to Ignore Error"

The Argument Advanced by Dr. Ferm

The ninth declaration of the cooperative Evangelists says that the Lord's "method of dealing with error was largely to ignore it."[1] Therefore, it is held, the lay Christian, the teacher, and the evangelist do not need to contend against the error of modernists and modernism; they merely should continue on proclaiming positive truth without reference to existing errors.

Dr. Ferm buttresses this opinion by the following words from the great evangelist, D. L. Moody.

> Christ's teaching was always constructive. He gave little attention to tearing down, because he knew that as light dispells darkness, so truth scatters error. His method of dealing with error was largely to ignore it, letting it melt away in the warm glow of the full intensity of truth expressed in love.[2]

An Examination of Dr. Ferm's Conclusions

Dr. Ferm is of the opinion that Christ's teaching was "always" constructive or helpfully upbuilding, and that Christ fought error chiefly by ignoring the error and by continuing to proclaim the positive truth without reference to the error. Naturally, *if* this is the actual method of Christ in combating *all* error, even the gravest of types such as that dealing with false prophets, then this ought to be the method of every present day Christian layman, teacher, and evangelist. This is precisely Dr. Ferm's conclusion.

The Writer's Critique

The method of cooperative evangelism is for the conservative speaker to *completely* and *entirely* ignore the error of liberalism,

---

1. *Ibid.*, pp. 39-40, quoting Dwight L. Moody, *The Watchman*, Nov. 8, 1899.
2. *Ibid.*

and to treat those on the sponsoring committees who are liberals as if they were fine brethren who teach the truth. Can this be defended on the grounds that the Lord's method of combating error was by generally ignoring it? In order to answer this some observations on Christ's procedure are here necessary.

It must first be observed that the Lord treated errors in more than one way, depending on the faith or faithlessness of the erring person and the negligibleness or gravity of the error and its effects. However, there is a uniform element in the Lord's treatment of error. This is the fact that He never gave His approval or sanction to the error. The fact that it was morally impossible for Him, being divine, to cooperate with or go along with error is the backbone of the rebuttal which conservatives give to liberals who in their advocacy of the Kenosis Theory contend that the Lord went along with many of the errors of His day. In view of this how can Dr. Ferm justify cooperative evangelism's giving the impression to the public that known liberals are religious worthies by allowing them to pray in the evangelistic service, by directing converts to their churches, and by speaking favorably of them in public?

It is difficult to cite individual errors which were *ignored* by the Lord, because who can point to an error and then claim that the Lord who had omniscient eyes and the mind of God never addressed Himself to it in His often sublime and subtle words of deep meaning. One can only at most declare on any particular error that he does not see where or when the Lord corrected it plainly, but who can declare that the Lord simply ignored it? To assert the truth in the face of an error, and thus correct it without mouthing the words, "I am now correcting such-and-such's error," is in fact to correct the error, and even this practice cannot be considered as "ignoring" the error. In any case the thesis that the Lord corrected errors largely by ignoring them cannot by the nature of the case readily be substantiated by a list of ignored errors. On the other hand the entire New Testament, including especially the Sermon on the Mount, Matthew 23, many of the parables, and the Lord's constant dialogue with His enemies as well as with His disciples provides countless instances of the Lord's correcting and rebuking errors of morality and doctrine.

The Lord's correction of various types of errors in different ways stands out in the New Testament. In John 11:40 Jesus is seen gently correcting Martha's error in protesting to the removal of the stone guarding Lazarus' tomb; in John 13:38 the Savior gently but firmly corrects Peter's error of self-confidence by foretelling to Peter his future threefold denial of his master; and numberless similar incidents could be tabulated which demonstrate Jesus' gentle but firm correction of the errors of His own flock. In John 16:12 Jesus tells the disciples, "I have many things to say unto you, but ye cannot bear them now," thus informing the reader that certain errors were not corrected at once, but the all-wise Christ looked for the most auspicious time to correct mistaken ideas. This usually was immediately after the error, but on some of the deeper theological concepts Christ waited until after the disciples had witnessed His resurrection.

In the famed Sermon on the Mount, which is cited by so many as the pure example of positive teaching in contrast to negativism, Christ repeatedly uses the formula, "Ye have heard . . . but I say unto you" (Matt. 5), and is seen to correct error after error which had crept into Rabbinical Judaism by directly citing the error, exposing its shortcoming, and by teaching the truth. In each of these sayings, as well as in others in Matthew 6 and 7, Christ is directly contradicting the teachings of erring Rabbis and is doing the very *opposite* of ignoring error!

The prime example of all, however, wherein the Lord did not ignore error was in His relations with the unbelieving hypocritical false prophets of His day. In Matthew 23 His severe denunciation of the errors of the Pharisees *and* of the Pharisees themselves wherein He cites them as children of hell (v. 15) and pronounces an eightfold "Woe" upon them, displays the opposite of one who *ignores* error! This is especially true in view of his citation of particular errors before each of His several denunciations. In Matthew 22:29 in the face of the Saducees' error concerning the resurrection the Lord did not declare that everyone has their own particular view on the topic, and then after paying His respects to the Saducean scholarship, proceed to "positively" give His own view *without* declaring that they erred. Instead His words began with the tones, "Ye de err." In John 2:13-17 and in

Matthew 21:12-13 Christ is seen cleansing the Temple both at the beginning and end of His ministry. This shows that in both the circumstances of inaugurating His earthly ministry and of concluding it the Saviour's inner being compelled Him to the identical action. He could, if His general practice was to ignore error and merely speak in a positive vein, have given a wonderful and moving exhortation as to the proper purpose and function of the Temple and as to the most suitable mode of pleasing God when in it. Instead, however, He attacked both the error and the errorists, exposing both for their wickedness, and then in the case of the second purification taught the true use of the Temple by quoting, "My house shall be called the house of prayer, . . ." (Matt. 21:13). The examinations of Christ's visits to the Temple and the Synagogue, previously dealt with in connection with Arguments III and IV, also revealed a Saviour who continually rebuked both error and errorists openly, clearly, and boldly. The evidence simply does not substantiate the assertion that Christ's method of combating error was to largely ignore it. In fact, this is seen to be quite the opposite of the truth *in the case* of Christ's dealings with the false religious teachers and leaders of His day.

Christ's teaching was "always constructive," as should be the teaching of today, in the sense that its final purpose was to increase and vindicate the glory and truth of God, to build His Church, and to have the sinner come face to face with his sin so that he might be converted! However, if "always constructive" refers to not condemning evil, not denouncing evildoers, not warning His own against false prophets, not upbraiding unbelief and unbelievers, not calling the Christ-rejecting unbelieving Pharisees names in righteous scorn, indignation, and wrath, then Christ's teaching was assuredly beyond all doubts *not* "always constructive." It is to be noted in passing that much of the Bible, including God's Decalogue, is not free from negativism.

Another point which needs to be noted is concerning Dr. Ferm's assertion that,

> Scriptural separation is positive and not negative. It is separation *to* something rather than separation *from* something.[3]

3. Ferm, p. 34.

Fundamentalists have no objection to these words, for the separatist position does not advocate mere separation from unbelievers followed by seclusion and retirement from the work of the Lord. However, Dr. Ferm's proper enunciation of the need for separtists to conduct evangelism and the other phases of the Lord's labor in addition to their contending for the faith, the truth of which the Separatists also acknowledge, in no way defends cooperative evangelism's posture of not only not contending for the faith, but also of aiding the modernist enemies of the Gospel. This is true in light of the ancient maxim that, "Obedience in one particular cannot atone for transgression in another."[4]

One final point needs to be mentioned. Despite the quotation of D. L. Moody which stated that the Lord's "method of dealing with error was largely to ignore it,"[5] Moody himself in his sermons, although he advanced the cooperative spirit, made constant references against deists, skeptics, infidels, false teachers, and false doctrines.[6] When asked regarding inclusive evangelism, "Is it right for any man or woman who has not been converted to have anything to do in an evangelical church?" he said, "I never set an unconverted man or woman to work, but Christian men need to be warmed up and then set to work to convert those who are not Christian."[7]

Conclusions

It has been noted, contrary to the assertion made in the proposition at hand, that it cannot be sustained that the Lord's method of dealing with error was largely to ignore it. In fact it has been seen that although the Lord gently corrected the errors of His own flock, in the case of the enemies of God and His truth on numerous occasions He publicly exposed, warned against, and sternly

---

4. Frederic W. Farrar, *The Life of Christ* (London: Cassell & Co., Ltd. 1887), p. 355.

5. Ferm, p. 40, quoting Moody, *The Watchman*, Nov. 8, 1899.

6. E.g., Dwight L. Moody, "Temptation," *Moody's Latest Sermons* (Chicago: Moody Press, 1900), p. 59, and Dwight L. Moody, "Come Thou and All Thy House into the Ark," *The Overcoming Life* (Chicago: Moody Press, 1896), p. 63.

7. William R. Moody, *The Life of Dwight L. Moody by His Son* (Chicago: Fleming H. Revell, 1900), p. 458.

rebuked the false teachers of Israel with righteous indignation. Thus the proposition which advocates that Christians and evangelists by following Christ's example ought to ignore the pernicious error of modernism, not warn against it, and not rebuke the false teachers, cannot be sustained on the basis of an examination of the gospel accounts of the Lord's ministry.

ARGUMENT X

"The Lord Was Never Concerned with Sponsorship"

The Argument Advanced by Dr. Ferm

The tenth item for debate is the assertion of the New Evangelical that "Sponsorship caused little or no concern on the part of Jesus and the apostles,"[1] and that therefore, the evangelist ought not to be distracted from his essential mission of proclaiming the Gospel by concerning himself with that which did not concern his Lord.[2]

An Examination of Dr. Ferm's Conclusions

Dr. Ferm's words unmistakably mirror the fact that he has concluded that the sponsorship question was never of any concern to the Lord and therefore should not be any concern to the evangelical preacher of today. He sees it as a distraction from the central mission of preaching the Gospel. This may be because concern over sponsorship is thought by him to limit the opportunity of preaching the Gospel by reducing the doctrinal latitude of the sponsoring parties and thus reducing the potential audience of the evangelist since each one on the sponsoring committee of a crusade usually causes many of his own constituents to attend the meetings.

The apparent effectiveness of Dr. Graham's ministry in winning souls apparently justifies in Dr. Ferm's eyes the practice of permitting known liberals to be on the sponsoring committee, his welcoming them, defending their presence, and according to them all the rights and privileges of any conservative sponsor including the leading in prayer and the participation in the other phases of the campaign.

---

1. Ferm., p. 31.
2 *Ibid.*

> Then said Jesus unto them, When ye have lifted up the Son of man, then shall ye know that I am he, and that I do nothing of myself; but as my Father hath taught me, I speak these things. And he that sent me is with me: the Father hath not left me alone; for I do always those things that please him (John 8:28,29).

The above words of Jesus indicate that His ultimate sponsor, the one who brought Him to the earth and the one whom He represented, was the Father. This should be true for every preacher of the Good Tidings. As for earthly sponsors, who would bring Christ into their region, be responsible for Him and His message, and stand with Him before the public in a common bond of fellowship, mutual approval, and unity, there do not appear to be any who did precisely this. Thus, Dr. Ferm's assertion that, "Sponsorship caused little or no concern on the part of Jesus . . .," seems to have some credibility in the limited sense that it does not appear that anyone or any group sponsored Jesus in the same way that a modern evangelist is sponsored.

However, before it can be concluded that Christ was not concerned with sponsorship, it must be determined whether or not He was concerned with some or all of the elements of which the modern sponsorship relation is composed. Thus with regard to the elements involved it is asked, "Was Christ unconcerned over the parties with whom He cooperated, fellowshipped, and gave approval?" "Was He unconcerned over the parties to whom He entrusted the care of part of His flock?" "Did He or would He ever make a tacit agreement not to rebuke false teachers, which is the agreement made by a conservative who accepts the invitation to hold meetings under liberal auspices?" The answers to all of these questions have already been studied in the nine previous propositions which inquired into these very matters. They uniformly were seen to be negative! He was not unconcerned!

The Saviour's continual open struggle against the religious leaders of His time with their pernicious rejection of Him and His redemption, which was noted earlier in Arguments III and IV, gives unanswerable evidence that Christ did not cooperate with just anyone! His continual public denunciations of the false prophets give ample evidence that Christ abhorred their errors of doctrine and ethics so thoroughly that it was impossible for anyone to think for a moment that He was cooperating with the Pharisees, Sadducees, rabbinical schools, or Herodians. Christ's complete isolation of His work and message from the errorists of His day is well brought out in Dr. Van Til's words,

> . . . However much they [the false leaders of Christ's time] disagreed among themselve on other matters they agreed on the idea of salvation by works or character. And they ruled in the one organization on earth raised up for the dissemination of the idea of salvation by grace. So, as they did not invite Jesus to cooperate in preaching their gospel with them so Jesus did not invite them to preach his gospel with him. *Jesus made provision for their removal* from their position of leadership among the people. The establishment of his kingdom was predicated on the destruction of theirs. Their house would be left desolate to them. "Woe unto you, scribes and Pharisees, hypocrites! for ye compass sea and land to make one proselyte, and when he is made, ye make him twofold more the child of hell than yourselves" (Matt. 23:15).[3]

Thus the Saviour's concern with the elements of sponsorship prove His concern with the basic relationship itself.

The basic error in the reasoning of Dr. Ferm lies in his affirmation that the Lord does not care about a relationship which exists today solely on the grounds that this same exact relationship is not *precisely* discernible in the New Testament. The New Testament pictures the missionary-evangelist constantly invading new territory with the truth by his own impetus, or with the added impetus of the church which sent him (Acts 13:3), rather than his being invited by parties already resident—as is the case in the present day when a group invites an evangelist to come into their region under their auspices. However, when this sponsorship relationship is analyzed, it is observed that the New Testament contains strong views on the subject of what flag a man of God may travel under and gives the example of Christ who never was seen under a soiled banner.

---

3. Van Til, *op. cit.*, pp. 26-27.

The following sentence of Dr. Ferm is also in need of comment.

> To distract a messenger seems to be the aim of some, in spite of the fact that the effectiveness of his ministry cannot be denied in the presence of multitudes of witnesses around the world.[4]

It is difficult to determine whether Dr. Ferm is here referring to the *criticism* concerning the sponsorship of Dr. Graham's meetings as the distracting element, or if he means that the actual *determining* who are and who are not proper sponsors would be the distracting element. He also may mean that the distraction would be the resultant reduction of liberal participation in the meetings, which would result in fewer of the liberal's adherents coming under the sound of the message of the evangelist. Thus a distraction of opportunity would be meant.

If he means the first, that the criticism is the distraction, then he misjudges the motives of the critics who are concerned greatly over God's Word, God's commands, the aid given to the rise of the liberals by his policies, and the welfare of Christ's little ones who are directed into the liberal churches. He then also misjudged the gravity of the issue, the division which cooperative evangelism has caused among conservatives, and the weight of the evidence which shows Christ at enmity with all that is false and untrue.

If he means the second, that it would be a distraction for the evangelist to occupy his time with sponsorship tests, then he errs on several counts, for (1) the question depends on whether or not the Scriptures reveal it as something which is *necessary* to be done, and not on what seems to be the wisest use of the evangelist's time as on a matter of option; (2) a sponsorship test in the form of a creedal statement to be signed would not take much of the evangelist's time; and (3) he minimizes the results which would be or would have been accomplished by time so spent, for it would unite conservatives, rebuke the modernists, and protect Christ's little ones.

---

4. Ferm, p. 31.

If the third alternative is intended, which looks upon the sponsorship issue as one which could reduce the numbers of liberals who come under the hearing of the Word, then again it must be affirmed that (1) the question is not what is expedient in man's sight, but what is right in God's sight; (2) whatever loss in liberal adherents that would occur could very well be compensated for by the gain of the estranged fundamentalists' adherents; and (3) the uniting of the conservative camp, the thwarting of the liberals, the protection of the lambs from the modernists, and the setting back of the ecumenical movement and modernism which might be accomplished by limiting the sponsorship to only conservative groups may in the over-all outreach of the Church more than equal the number of converts brought in through the present methods.

Despite Dr. Ferm's comments on the unchallenged effectiveness of the ministry of cooperative evangelism in Dr. Graham's case, the supreme Judge in heaven may yet some day reveal to him that if the sponsorship had been limited to fundamentalists, humanly speaking, thousands upon thousands more might have been converted. If not in crusades, in the over-all outreach of the Church throughout the globe. Until that future day when the righteous Judge declares upon the relative effectiveness of cooperative evangelism compared to the damage it has done to the outreach of Christ because of its approval of the liberals, and compared to what might have been, this point will have to be held in abeyance. However, it can surely be said now, that despite apparent results and regardless of what opportunities any expert may think are to be lost, God's work cannot be done in any better way than in God's way.

Conclusions

It has been noted that Christ did not have any earthly sponsor which was directly responsible for inviting Him to come to a region with His message and which cooperated with Him in a united mutually approving front before the people. Yet because He displayed in His ministry a clear line of demarcation from all semblances of error in doctrine or conduct and their proponents, rebuking them and their false teachings constantly, it cannot be

76

sustained that He was not concerned with whom He cooperated or with whom He was thought to have cooperated. Thus, since the elements of cooperation and mutual approval are part of the sponsorship relation, it is seen that Christ in His concern over these would also be and in fact now is vitally concerned with the sponsorship of the message and messengers which go forth in His name.

In view of the evidence, the tenth proposition which affirms that Christ is not now concerned with the question of sponsorship must be regarded as untrue.

SUMMARY AND CONCLUSION

Dr. Ferm's Interpretation Errs

Dr. Graham's volume, *Cooperative Evangelism: Is Billy Graham Right or Wrong?* defends the inclusivist policy on the grounds of the Bible and the ministries of the successful evangelists of the last two and one-half centuries. The defense of his views based on the ministry of the Lord was the only area analyzed in this thesis, but the same arguments may be seen to pervade all of Dr. Ferm's biblical interpretation, and if his arguments based on the Saviour's ministry are sound, the case will no doubt also carry in his other biblically based sections; however, if the reasoning and conclusions here are spurious, the same verdict will have to be rendered over his other thrusts. This is true because Dr. Ferm is arguing over a *trend* in Scripture which concerns the treatment of a group of God's enemies—those who claim to be prophets of Jehovah, but who reject the Jehovah of the Prophets, i.e., the modernists.

The verdict of this study in view of our analysis of Dr. Ferm's book in the light of the Bible, is that he has erred in interpreting the basic attitude of Christ toward God's enemies. Thus his conclusions and reasonings, although sincerely made in an effort to serve God, are incorrect. It is the opinion of the writer that Dr. Ferm's key assertion, "Jesus himself affords us the best example of cooperation [i.e., with errorists],"[1] has not been established in his book. Such a view cannot be sustained on the basis of the New Testament, and cannot be rightly applied to cooperative evangelists in order to justify their cooperation with liberal elements. In fact, it is the conclusion of this study that the Lord's ministry argues for the exact opposite of cooperative evangelism by virtue of Christ's unceasing acrimonious struggle with the unbelieving false religious leaders of His day whom He continually publicly rebuked and warned against. His open and increasing hostility to them cannot possibly be used to prove anything except that Christians

---

1. Ferm, p. 36.

78

are to likewise openly rebuke and warn against false prophets. Christ's cooperation, fellowship, and approval was confined to only those who professed to be His; and His dealing with sinners was always characterized by His proclaiming the truth, correcting the errors, and by the Saviour's complete freedom from ever giving an outward appearance of approval of, fellowship with, or cooperation with false teachers, unbelievers, or evildoers. This is far different from the posture of cooperative evangelism which not only fails to rebuke the false teachers, but which cooperates with them and honors them as "Brethren."

Concerning Dr. Ferm's appeal to the methodology of the evangelists it may be noted that the ministries of the great evangelists, or their teachings, are not really the place to determine what the Bible teaches about a particular subject. God blessed the labors of these men because of their untiring energy in proclaiming the true Gospel to multitudes of men, because of the work of the Holy Spirit, the unseen prayers of countless Christians, and of the faithful planting done by others in thousands upon thousands of cases where the evangelists reaped. Their good results do not make them infallible teachers. This can especially be seen to be true when one considers that unlike the Bible, they disagreed among themselves. Who would question the fact that John Wesley would vigorously stand against Finney's denial of the sinful nature of man?[2] Let the Lord be praised for the use He made made of these great men, but for infallible teaching the Scriptures alone are to be sought out. It must also be noted that homilies which the evangelists primarily deal with, are not identical with commentaries: the one having a hortatory thrust, the other an exegetical one. In addition to all of this, the conclusion that the evangelists of the past present a unified case in favor of cooperative evangelism is open to no little question.

2. Charles G. Finney, *Lectures on Systematic Theology* (South Gate: Colporter Kemp, 1878), pp. 251-53.

Dr. Ferm's sundry assertions concerning Christ's ministry and its justification of the neo-evangelical inclusivist stance were divided by this writer into ten basic arguments or claims. Each one stated an alleged characteristic of Christ's ministry which Dr. Ferm advanced in his book, and its alleged or implied application toward the justification of cooperative evangelism.

The first argument affirmed that Christ's instructions to the twelve and the seventy gave them warrant to abide with *anyone* at all, and therefore the modern evangelist could do likewise. However, it was seen that Christ in Matthew 10:11 commanded the twelve to search out a host who was *worthy, axios*. This command eliminates known heathen and false teachers, and negates the alleged claim that Christ instructed His disciples to abide with or cooperate with *any* at all who would be comparable to liberals.

The second argument affirmed that Christ accepted cooperation from any who did not oppose Him, and that today's preachers may do likewise. Here, however, it was found that this assertion could be made only by improperly defining the word "oppose," so that today's unbelieving liberals could be understood not to oppose the cause of Christ. When unbelief and indifference to the claims of Christ and to the facts concerning His life, and the teaching of same, were also included as they should be as forms of opposition, it was seen that it was impossible to assert that Christ ever accepted or would have accepted the cooperation of any who so erred. It was seen that the biblical picture of those who do not oppose Christ, was that of those who are for Him and His claims. These, who could not be liberals who reject the historicity of so much of the Bible's Christ, are those who are truly Christian; and these are the ones whose cooperation Christ accepts and seeks.

The third and fourth argument maintained that Christ cooperated with errorists by His Temple and Synagogue attendance respectively, and therefore the preacher of today could enter houses of error and need not withdraw from the errorists. Here the defense of inclusivist evangelism could not be substantiated because of the great difference between the conduct of Christ in the Temple and the synagogue and the behavior of the cooperative evangelist in the meetings which have modernists on the sponsoring committee. That difference lies in the fact that a complete study of Jesus' Temple and synagogue visits revealed that He continually outspokenly and scornfully rebuked and reproved publicly the Christ-denying religious hypocrites of His day. He did not allow their errors to obtain His approval, but warned the people publicly and plainly against them. The cooperative evangelist on the other hand differs completely from the Lord by his silence before error and his failure to warn the flock against the Christ-denying modernists. His approval of the errorists has no parallel in Christ's visits to the house of worship in Israel.

The fifth argument avers on the grounds of Christ engaging in contact and conversation with the religious rejects of His day that the conservative Christian preacher can engage in cooperation with the religious rejects of this age. However, it was observed that Christ always dealt with the errors of the religious rejects whom He went among, and never gave the impression that He was cooperating with them or seeking their aid to accomplish His divine purposes. In contrast to this the neo-evangelical evangelist gives approval to and seeks aid from the modernists with whom he cooperates. Thus Christ's conduct in this area cannot be used logically to justify the behavior of the orthodox preacher who is sponsored by modernists, for Christ *went to* the rejects with news of salvation, He did not *come with* them to others.

The sixth argument declares that the Lord specifically forbade Christians from sitting in judgment concerning which of those who wish to sponsor his campaigns are sound and which are not. Upon a study of Matthew 7:1 in its context which commands, "Judge not, that ye be not judged," and an examination of the entire subject of "judging" as it is found in the Scripture and as it has been understood by commentators, it was discovered that the judging which Christ forbade was the censorious hypercriticalness which characterized the hypocrites who saw the small faults of others but who overlooked their own unmercifulness. The judging of the doctrinal orthodoxy of others was not

81

only seen not to be prohibited, but was observed to be the clear duty of a Christian in order for him to carry out the commands of Christ among which is the imperative to "Beware of false prophets" (Matt. 7:15).

The seventh and eighth arguments concern the alleged stress of the Lord's ministry. The seventh affirms that the ministry of the Saviour emphasized the evil of hypocrisy rather than the error of incorrect theology. However, it was noted through a study of the New Testament usage of "hypocrisy" that the Pharisees were the target of this denunciation by Christ, and that their hypocrisy was inextricably woven together with their unbelief in Christ, so that in the Saviour's denunciation of the "hypocrites" of His day, He was also condemning the Christ-rejecting unbelievers. It was also noted that His denunciation of the Pharisee's hypocrisy does not conflict with, but coincides with His denunciation of unbelief in His Messiahship, which is the cornerstone of false doctrine. The using of these facts to defend silence in the face of Christ-rejecting hypocritical liberals, who justify themselves on the basis of ethical achievement and a non-substitutionary atonement, was seen to be a *non sequitur*.

The eighth argument which averred that the Lord's ministry stressed fellowship rather than separation was rejected as a defense for cooperative evangelism after it was observed that the fellowship emphasized by Christ was that of brethren with brethren, in contrast to that of brethren with unbeliever. Between brethren and unbeliever separation is the New Testament stress as well as the stress of Christ's years upon earth.

The ninth argument stated that the Lord's method of dealing with error was largely to ignore it, and therefore the method of cooperative evangelism which overlooks the errors of the liberals was correct in contrast to the separatist method of rebuking and warning. Here it was noted that Christ dealt with various errors in different ways. He waited until the propitious time to correct certain misunderstandings of His disciples which had to await His resurrection to be understood. While He was gentle and long-suffering in correcting the errors of His own flock, He rebuked publicly the false teachers. In no case can it be substantiated with certainty that Christ dealt with error by *ignoring* it; for Christ's correction sometimes is too subtle for mortal eyes to view and sometimes it may be delayed, but who can with certainty maintain the negative, that in such-and-such a case it did not come? Thus in view of this, and in view of Christ's public and unceasing struggle with the errors of the unbelieving religious leaders of His era, the ignoring of the errors of the modernists at the expense of the little lambs who get no food and who are led astray cannot be defended.

The tenth and final argument maintains that sponsorship should be no concern of the conservative of today because it was no concern to Christ. This was rejected on the grounds that the elements of cooperation and mutual approval inherent in the sponsorship relation was and is a very real concern to God and to Christ. Despite the precise sponsorial situation not occurring in Christ's ministry as it does in the case of a modern, Christ's concern with the associations and associates of His message and messenger more than establish His concern for the sponsorship of that which goes forth in His name.

Conclusion

From the study of the Bible which has now been accomplished it can only be concluded that New Evangelicalism and its evangelical method, Cooperative [with the liberal neo-orthodox theologians] Evangelism, are not supported by the words and deeds of the Saviour, but rather they are boldly and clearly refuted by Christ. Thus the ten arguments for Cooperative Evangelism here analyzed actually provide a clear claim on every true Christian's conscience for biblical separation from all heretics and apostates in doing the work of the Lord. Let all constantly remember that, "God's work must be done in God's way."